D0710388

TOWARDS A HISTORY OF ADULT EDUCATION IN AMERICA

CROOM HELM SERIES ON THEORY AND PRACTICE OF
ADULT EDUCATION IN NORTH AMERICA
Edited by Peter Jarvis, University of Surrey

TOWARDS A HISTORY OF ADULT EDUCATION IN AMERICA

The Search for a Unifying Principle

HAROLD W. STUBBLEFIELD

CROOM HELM
London • New York • Sydney

© 1988 H.W. Stubblefield
Croom Helm Ltd, Provident House, Burrell Row,
Beckenham, Kent, BR3 1AT

Croom Helm Australia, 44-50 Waterloo Road,
North Ryde, 2113, New South Wales

Published in the USA by
Croom Helm
in association with Methuen, Inc.
29 West 35th Street
New York, NY 10001

British Library Cataloguing in Publication Data

Stubblefield, Harold W.
    Towards a history of adult education in
    America: the search for a unifying
    principle. — (Croom Helm series on theory
    and practice of adult education in
    North America)
    1. Adult education — United States —
    History — 20th century
    I. Title
    374'.973   LC5251
    ISBN 0-7099-4463-2

Library of Congress Cataloging-in-Publication Data

ISBN 0-7099-4463-2

**Printed and bound in Great Britain
by Billing & Sons Limited, Worcester.**

CONTENTS

Contents

EDITOR'S NOTE

The Croom Helm Series of books on the Theory and Practice of Adult Education in North America provides scholars and students with a collection of studies by eminent scholars on all aspects of adult education throughout the whole continent. This series includes books on all the sub-disciplines of adult education including: history, philosophy, sociology, etc. They will cover both theoretical and practical considerations and each is a major contribution to its own specific field. Some of these studies are symposia while others are single authored treatises.

This book is one of the earliest in this series and it is an excellent historical study of the second quarter of this century, an important time for American adult education as it was beginning to become established and accepted throughout the land. This study by Harold Stubblefield charts this process and brings to life the people who had a great deal of influence on the directions that adult education took during this period. Additionally, he highlights some of the significant thinkers, who are often un-appreciated by adult educators in the United States at the present time because of a preoccupation with the present, both in ideas and in practice.

There are many other books planned in this series, including some more historical studies, which will continue to provide opportunity for the theory and practice of adult education in North America to be explored in both an academic and a practical manner.

Peter Jarvis
(Series Editor)

To
Paul Bergevin
John McKinley
H. Mason Atwood
George K. Gordon
Walton Connelly

Bureau of Studies in Adult Education
Indiana University
1969-1970

ACKNOWLEDGEMENTS

This book is dedicated to the five persons who were the faculty of the Bureau of Studies in Adult Education at Indiana University when I began doctoral studies in 1969. They were Paul Bergevin, John McKinley, H. Mason Atwood, George K. Gordon, and Walton Connelly. When I defended my dissertation in the fall of 1972, only Begevin and McKinley remained on the faculty, and Bergevin had officially retired the previous spring.

My intellectual debt to Bergevin is considerable. Bergevin had been deeply influenced by the community organization approach of the American Association for Adult Education and the adult education philosophy of Eduard Lindeman, Harry Overstreet, and N.F.S. Grundtvig, founder of the Danish folk high school. These influences are obvious in Bergevin's philosophy of adult education and in Participation Training, the training design he developed with his younger colleague, John McKinley. McKinley directed my dissertation research in which I first explored some of the ideas treated in this book and encouraged me in my first graduate teaching assignment. I regard Paul Bergevin and John McKinley as my mentors in adult education.

In 1977 when I had just begun to explore some research ideas in the history of American adult education, Alexander Charters of Syracuse University through funds at his disposal supported two one-week visits in the summer to study the adult education collection at the George Arents Research Library and the E.S. Bird Library. From that Syracuse experience came my first experience in a research library and the idea for a book on the development of adult education in the 1920s and 1930s. I am grateful for his encouragement.

Several persons provided assistance with this book for whose help I am most grateful. During the early stages of the research, my son, Hugh, and my daughter, Carol, located sources on several of the persons examined in this book. Gerald Cline and Leroy Miles, colleagues at Virginia Tech, read and commented on the manuscript. My wife, Betty, read the entire manuscript and offered helpful suggestions. My daughter, Carol, critiqued a draft and suggested changes for clarity and grammatical correctness. I am particularly indebted to David Stewart for his assessment and critique. Beyond his helpfulness with editorial matters, he also saved me from errors of fact, particularly in the chapter on Lindeman. Norma McGehee, my secretary, provided invaluable assistance during the final stages of manuscript preparation by editing the manuscript, typing the end notes in proper form, and printing the final draft.

INTRODUCTION

In the United States prior to World War I, a national - not federal - system of adult education was in place. Adults learned through chautauquas, lyceum lectures, correspondence schools, university extension, agricultural programs, women's organizations, service clubs, and programs sponsored by voluntary associations. New agencies for the education of adults had mushroomed before the war, often under the impetus of national organizations and national social movements whose units or activities extended into American communities.

After Word War I many persons and institutions in the United States made adult education their business, and they used these educational activities to serve almost every conceivable interest. The term adult education was widely used as the covering term for a wide variety of activities that served propaganda and profit-making as well as educational purposes. Many persons used the term adult education as a label for their activities simply because the term was in vogue. They were unaware of any deeper and non-institutional meaning that the term might have had.

The term adult education did, indeed, have a deeper meaning for many. During and after the war many persons began to grapple in thoughtful and disciplined ways with the question of what kind of education adults needed. Educators, intellectuals, foundation executives, and civic leaders addressed the issue of how American citizens - the educated middle class and working class - could be equipped to cope with the new social order brought about by World War I and its aftermath, the explosion of new knowledge and the separation of the expert from lay persons, the threat to democracy from totalitarianism abroad and repression at home, and the new economic and social conditions created by the impact of urbanization and industrialization.

More than just promoting the extension of educational opportunities to greater numbers of adults, they asked basic questions about what adult education ought to be. They searched for coherence, for some answer to the question of what kind of education adults should have. These persons were the first generation theorists of adult education as a social practice. Some of these theorists are well-known even today, while others will be recognized only by persons with a specialist's knowledge of the literature of adult education.

Among others, they include James Harvey Robinson, Herbert Croly, Alvin S. Johnson, William S. Learned, Frederick P. Keppel, Morse A. Cartwright, Dorothy Canfield Fisher, Edward L. Thorndike, Lyman Bryson, Everett Dean Martin, Robert M. Hutchins, Mortimer J. Adler, Alexander Meiklejohn, John Walker Powell, Joseph K. Hart, Eduard C. Lindeman, and Harry A. Overstreet. As to occupation, they were university professors and presidents, foundation and associational executives, journal editors, administrators of adult education institutions, lecturers, writers, researchers, and social activists.

Considered collectively, they were the first generation theorists of the adult education movement in the United States. Their writings on adult education were diverse, often episodic and unsystematic. Some wrote prolifically and some little. Some worked in adult education as a full-time career, but for others adult education was only one interest among many.

They addressed basic issues about the nature of adult education, the social conditions which called for new forms of education, the aims to be accomplished, the methods most appropriate for accomplishing these aims, the relation of adult education to society, and what the content should be. In addressing these issues, they appeared to work within what I have called a unifying principle. Within the perspective of these unifying principles they made their diagnosis of the adult educational needs that were unmet by the opportunities available then. From the values inherent in these unifying principles they also made their educational prescription.

For one group of theorists the unifying principle was the diffusion of knowledge and culture. Major representatives of this principle treated in this book are James Harvey Robinson and other founders of the New School for Social Research, persons associated with the Carnegie Corporation's experiment in adult education through the American Association for Adult Education, and Lyman Bryson.

For another group, the unifying principle was liberal education. Major representatives were Everett Dean Martin of the People's Institute of New York City, Robert M. Hutchins and Mortimer J. Adler who founded the Great Books program for adults, and Alexander Meiklejohn and John Walker Powell who pioneered in adult reading groups.

A third group worked within the unifying principle of social education. Joseph K. Hart and Eduard C. Lindeman regarded adult education as a form of applied social science, and Harry Overstreet, a philosopher, derived from the social sciences a determinative concept to assess individual and institutional behavior.

Their own published materials have been used as the major sources for this book. Some of their publications on adult education began to appear in the second decade of this century; their major works, for the most part, appeared in the twenties and thirties; for others such as Bryson, Overstreet, and Powell, their most mature treatments were not published until the late forties and early fifties. The source material was not restricted to adult education publications. Examining their non-adult educational publications was important, particularly so in the cases of James Harvey Robinson, Lyman Bryson, Everett Dean Martin, Alexander Meiklejohn, Joseph K. Hart, Eduard C. Lindeman, and Harry Overstreet. Adult education became for them the sphere of action in which they worked out their intellectual and social agendas.

Their agendas for adult education are now one or two generations removed from the contemporary situation. Beginning in the sixties, new paradigms of education began to emerge. Unesco works within the framework of lifelong education, the Organization for Economic Cooperation and Development operates within the framework of recurrent education, and the paradigm in the United States - not yet fully articulated - appears to be organized around a loosely defined idea of lifelong learning. The first generation theorists, for all their differences, identified non-vocational adult roles as the core problem for adult education to address. The vocational training and educational needs were, they believed, adequately served through existing programs. The reverse is true today. Interest in the vocation of adults as citizens which engaged these early theorists has greatly diminished. How to equip adults for their place in the economic sector now engages the greatest interest.

Changes in emphasis are necessary responses to changing social conditions. New forms of adult education evolve to address unmet learning needs as the needs are manifested in various domains of human activity. New terms are coined to describe these new forms. These new forms require specialized personnel to provide leadership and to conduct daily operations.

In every generation there are those who address issues about the education of adults that transcend specific institutional, content, or clientele concerns. Every social science discipline and social practice - adult education included - evolves in response to some 'problematic', to some new condition in society, that requires new forms of knowledge and new ways of helping persons to understand and respond to those conditions.

In the United States in the 1920s and 1930s, adult education emerged as a social practice focused around the 'problematic' of adult learning needs. Using adult education as a normative term, this first generation of theorists proposed different solutions, for they identified the learning need differently. This first generation of theorists were articulate, and their written products constitute the early classics of adult education. It would be a mistake to regard these products simply as the literature of a 'golden age' to which one retreats for wisdom and inspiration. It would also be a mistake to regard them as merely 'period pieces' important for what they reveal about how persons thought in that time.

The interpretations of this first generation of theorists remain important to contemporary adult educators for many reasons, but the most important is this. These theorists defined, for the first time, what adult education should be as a separate sphere of action in American society. In doing so, they defined the nature and range of problems that came under the province of adult education, and they defined the nature and range of the solutions appropriate through the agency of adult education. All of us whose interest transcends our particular segment of this enterprise and who search for a unifying principle for adult education conduct our inquiry within or in reaction against the tradition

Introduction

created by these theorists.

Part I

ADULT EDUCATION AS DIFFUSION OF KNOWLEDGE

Chapter One

THE NEW SCHOOL FOR SOCIAL RESEARCH, JAMES HARVEY ROBINSON, AND THE HUMANIZING OF KNOWLEDGE

By the beginning of World War I, universities had established a role in adult education. In 1914, the Smith-Lever Act established the federal Cooperative Extension Service as an agricultural extension function of the land-grant universities in each state. By 1916 the general extension work of universities had become so well established that the leaders organized the National University Extension Association. The mission of each of these forms of extension was to disseminate knowledge produced by research to serve the needs of professional groups and the adult lay public. In these new initiatives, universities were responding to several developments in American society, but one development made extension work both possible and necessary: the emergence of specialists who conducted research in small, defined segments of knowledge organized into disciplines.

In 1919 the New School for Social Research opened in New York City. For almost three-quarters of a century, the New School for Social Research has been recognized as a leading example of adult education for the educated. In its founding the New School represented the great hope for social reconstruction of two liberal journalists of the New Republic - Herbert Croly and Alvin S. Johnson - and several faculty members at Columbia University - Charles A. Beard, John Dewey, Wesley C. Mitchell, and James Harvey Robinson. Thorstein Veblen joined the group from the University of Missouri. The founders of the New School created an educational outpost of liberal thought and social reform, an institution of higher learning for educated lay persons. For a brief time they joined together in this

3

venture in adult education, creating a new school for conducting and disseminating social research.

The importance of the New School in the history of the early adult education movement in the United States is not confined to the educational opportunities it provided for adults in New York City. The founders grappled with fundamental questions: How can adults gain understanding of knowledge about the social order? Under what institutional auspices can such knowledge be produced and disseminated to the adult lay public? What should be the social purposes of this new adult education?

THE UNIVERSITY BECOMES A HOSTILE ENVIRONMENT

The precipitating event that focused the attention of the Columbia faculty on the possibility of a new 'university' was the firing in 1917 of three professors for their reported criticisms of the United States intervention in the war in Europe. Beard resigned in protest. This episode was one of several that convinced Beard that the university was controlled by trustees who were reactionary and without standing in education. Dewey, Robinson, and another professor protested the firing in the press, but the rest of the faculty did not protest.

These events at Columbia were part of a larger, unresolved issue over 'the nature, function, and social value of higher learning in America'. (1) At Columbia, several issues collided: patriotism and commitment to the war effort, academic freedom, and the bureaucratization of the university under a strong President and Board of Trustees.

By 1900 the universities, for the most part, had changed. Knowledge had been professionalized by the emergence of scholarly disciplines and the development of the academic profession. Specialists were trained in universities and inculcated with the importance of research. Associations of scholars were organized to define standards of higher learning. These professional associations replaced the pre-Civil War learned societies that had local membership open to everyone and were comprehensive in scope. Academic centers once open to cultivated men of letters now required special training. (2)

Silva and Slaughter point out that in this transition from the 'old' social scientist to the 'new' social scientist, a new relationship developed with the university. (3) The 'old' social scientists followed the traditional style of scholarship, namely, they possessed few books and few arguments which they applied to many situations. The modern social science required new resources for libraries, data sources, and data storage. Silva and Slaughter described this process as 'the industrialization of social science' and 'the bureaucratic organization of knowledge production'. Professors depended on university managers to get these resources. The academic 'craftsman' no longer owned the tools of his trade. Expertise had to be filtered through university managers and support secured from persons with resources, i.e., political leaders and private donors. An infrastructure was needed because the social scientist could no longer work alone.

Because the roles of the 'new' social scientists were defined by their dependence upon the university, they could not stray too far to the left or to the right. Expert service was used to establish multiple resource exchanges with the corporate center. The 'new' social scientists constructed an 'ideological center aligned with the emerging economic center.' They used professional associations such as the American Economic Association to define the nature and scope of the expert role.

The 'public role of men of knowledge' in the United States became a problem in World War I. In this war the universities, scholarship, and professors were now highly developed and considered a resource to be used. As Gruber (4) noted, the university in its modern form had joined with a technological war. Many university professors subordinated their role of disinterested scholarship to their role of patriotic citizens serving their country. Professors were in a problematic situation. To respond to the needs of the country, to be instruments of the government, threatened their integrity, but they could not refuse. They were trapped, as Gruber (5) said, in trying to maintain the thin line between society and the state.

The founders of the New School agreed that a 'new' university was needed. They wanted to combine advocacy and objectivity, a position they believed Columbia University prevented them from taking. Social scientists needed to be freed from restrictive universities and to organize research around social problems, not disciplines. Only this way, it seemed to them, could lead to social reconstruction.

THE MEN OF THE NEW SCHOOL: A NEW AMERICAN INTELLIGENTSIA

When considered individually, the founders of the New School of Social Research had remarkable careers. When considered collectively they constituted, with others, a new American intelligentsia who interpreted American life and institutions and the academic disciplines in more realistic terms than the genteel tradition. Genteel thought - formalist thought - had been entrenched for more than two generations. Hofstadter (6) described it as abstract, conservative, and with strong internal coherence in its arguments. Persons in the genteel tradition dealt with timeless varieties, but they were weak in describing reality and they could not deal with changing times.

Four of the major figures in what Morton White called a 'revolt against formalism' were James Harvey Robinson, Charles A. Beard, John Dewey, and Thorstein Veblen. (7) These academicians - the counterpart of the muckraking journalists and the naturalistic writers - attempted to get at 'reality'. In particular, the new social scientists believed that social conditions could only be explained by going back in time. Only historical explanations sufficed when all things were related and all things changed. In studying social problems, the relevant materials for explanations and solutions were to be derived from the social sciences. (8) They believed that knowledge provided the basis for social action and that ideas were 'modes of adjustment, plans of action.' (9)

James Harvey Robinson challenged the idea of history as the chronicle of the past, particularly of military and political events. (10) He made history a pragmatic weapon to explain the past and control the future. He called this approach the 'new history'. In 1895 he began his career at Columbia University where he stayed until his resignation in 1919 to begin the New School. Robinson believed that a study of history could explain the problems of the present. In a textbook written with Charles Beard, they announced their aim as helping modern readers understand their own times so that they would be able to understand the foreign news in the morning newspaper.

At the time the New School was formed, John Dewey was perhaps the premier American philosopher of education. His philosophy of instrumentalism held that ideas were plans of action, problems were solved by the methods of intelligence, and philosophy was concerned with social engineering, not metaphysics. Dewey taught at the University of Michigan and the University of Chicago before coming to Columbia in 1905. At Chicago he began research in education, established, with his wife, the University Elementary School, and published in 1899 The School and Society. Democracy and Education, his classic work on educational philosophy which influenced the early adult education movement, presented a conception of education as a process of growth and continuous through life.

Charles A. Beard, an eminent historian, related the economic interests of the founding fathers to the constitution, treating in a new way the presence of factions in democratic society and the protection of property as a source of factions and motivator for political behavior. While studying at Oxford University in England, he joined with Walter Vrooman, a young American, to start in 1899 a college called Ruskin Hall to provide education for the working class. In 1902 Beard and his wife returned to the United States where he entered doctoral studies at Columbia University. He received his Ph.D. in 1904 and joined the Columbia faculty in the department of political science. He continued his interest in public affairs, serving as a consultant to the New York Bureau of Municipal Research and participating in the National Municipal League.

Thorstein Veblen's institutionalism established the connections between economic institutions and other aspects of culture. Now called one of the leading social critics of his day, Veblen did not experience much success during his life. Veblen was an unsuccessful academician, a failure more for his unconventional lifestyle and flaunting of mores than his unorthodox ideas. He challenged conventional standards, pointing out their hollowness. His critique of higher education in The Higher Learning of America provided the blueprint for the organization of the New School. Undergraduate education for personal and cultural development should be separated from graduate education, he claimed, for the two could not exist in the same university. University faculty should do research and train graduate students.

Wesley C. Mitchell made major contributions to the scientific study of economics, pioneering in the use of quantitative analysis of the economy. He joined the Columbia University faculty in 1913, a position he held until

1944 except for three years he taught at the New School for Social Research. Mitchell believed in the importance of national organizations concerned with scientific research. He helped to organize and was active in the National Bureau of Economic Research and the Social Science Research Council.

Herbert Croly, the founder and editor of the New Republic, and Alvin Johnson his associate, were the other founders of the New School. Born in New York City in 1869, Croly's parents were David Goodman Croly, an exponent of the positivism of Auguste Comte, and Jane Cunningham Croly, a well-known journalist and founder of the women's club movement. He attended Harvard University and had an early career as a writer and editor. In 1905 he turned his attention to the social reforms initiated by the progressive movement and sought to provide an intellectual undergirding for them. This labor resulted in The Promise of American Life; its publication in 1909 established his reputation as 'the leading political philosopher in the United States'. (11) Willard Straight and his wife, Dorothy Whitney Straight, read Croly's book while they were in China. The book so impressed them that they looked Croly up on their return to New York City. In conversations over the next year or so, they learned of Croly's interest in publishing a weekly journal of opinion. Dorothy Straight promised to find the money, and Croly began to plan. The result was the New Republic that began publication in 1914 just as the war in Europe broke out.

Alvin Johnson had roots in midwestern agrarian and labor reform movements. In 1901 Johnson received his doctorate in economics from Columbia University and became a peripatetic professor - teaching briefly at several universities - until he came to the New Republic. In 1914 when the New Republic began publication and Johnson still taught at Cornell, Croly invited Johnson to New York for an interview and asked him to submit articles, editorials, and book reviews. The next year Croly invited Johnson to join the editorial staff, and Johnson took leave from Cornell to do so.

GOOD MEN COULD NOT AGREE

The New School for Social Research was organized during the Christmas holidays of 1918 and opened for classes in the spring of 1919. The New School opened successfully. Students and liberal professors were drawn to a school led by such distinguished liberal scholars as Beard and Robinson. The founders had agreed that the new educational institution would feature a lecture program, but, in reality, no resolution had been made about the School's purpose. The Croly faction wanted an emphasis on practical social change, and the Beard and Robinson faction wanted an emphasis on scientific and philosophic research.

In the initial agreement, each faction got enough of what it wanted to be satisfied. The lecture program satisfied Robinson and Johnson. Beard got three research fellows, and Mitchell expected to develop a research center in social and economic statistics. The favorable reaction toward his project for a Labor Research Bureau satisfied Croly. (12) Robinson (13) believed that these two tendencies were not in conflict, but the unfolding of events proved how badly he had misjudged the intensity of the feelings.

The lecture program adopted by the New School conformed more closely to the ideas of the Beard-Robinson faction: emphasis on the educational needs of adult learners and not on social change. After the New School had opened, Robinson in School and Society made clear his understanding of the New School as an institution of higher learning. The New School differed in its approach from the traditional public school and university emphasis on teaching. New School students typically were adults who had had some experiences in life, and by studying subjects in which they had an interest they were able to expand and interpret that experience. Because the learners already had the need to learn, the teachers did not have to stimulate it.

Not only did the learners differ, but the principle for organizing the courses differed. By restricting courses to the study of man and his predicament, human conduct, and social organization, and by not setting them off as disciplines within departments, the organization had been greatly simplified. In addition, the New School differed also in the 'scientific frankness' with which social issues could be studied. As an adult education institution, the New School did not have to protect the morals of the young or shield them from ideas that adults considered unsafe or too radical for young minds to hear. The New School excluded no social conditions, ideas, or thinkers from investigation.

The two factions did agree on basic ideas about this New School which they had created. First, as a bedrock belief, the founders believed in developing the social sciences into instruments of social progress - a basic principle of pragmatism - and they did not think that universities would permit this. In 1920 Mitchell explained to some friends how the New School operated and his reasons for leaving Columbia University to join this experiment. He called the New School part of a movement 'to apply the methods of science to the guidance of public affairs.' (14) This movement had produced other organizations, among them the Harvard Committee on Economic Research, the Bureau of Industrial Research, and the National Bureau of Economic Research. The efforts of these organizational creators had been supported by a hope, if not an assumption, that social inventions would emerge to control the new world created by mechanical inventions.

The social sciences were suspect, Mitchell argued, because they dealt with controversial issues about which many segments of society differed. The problem was made more difficult because of the organization of the university. Private schools had retired, conservative business men as trustees and depended on wealthy people for gifts. Public universities depended on legislatures which tended to be conservative. As a consequence, academic freedom, as the war experience at Columbia showed, could be limited.

When this occurred, new institutions such as the New School had to be formed to conduct research about social problems without constraint from political and economic interests. Contrary to common perceptions about the New School, the faculty, from the beginning, conducted research and regarded that activity as important, perhaps more important, than lecturing. The New School started with a core of full-time faculty members, and these independent scholars saw themselves as members of a club. They were committed to the reconstruction of society and to training men and women to carry on research in government and social organizations.

When Mitchell came to the New School, he had believed that doing social research with university students was difficult. These students could do some technical work, but they lacked significant practical experience for serious investigation. In the New School, an apprenticeship approach was adopted in which a student learned research skills from a scholar just as a young person learned from a master artisan. (15) When Mitchell left the New School and returned to Columbia three years later, he had changed his mind. He believed then that graduate students who were becoming professional economists would be able to advance economics as a science more than New School students.

The New School founders were not successful in achieving their goals for social reconstruction. As an institution for social reconstruction, the New School was untimely born. The climate for reform generated by the progressive movement before the war had given way to repression and suspiciousness of anything foreign during the war. Soon after the war in 1919-1920, a period of severe repressive activity known as the 'Red Scare' swept the country. In this period of national hysteria, people were arrested and deported and the print media censored. Liberals such as James Harvey Robinson and John Dewey were called 'parlor' Reds and Thorstein Veblen was considered radical. Journals of liberal opinion, including the New Republic, were accused of supporting revolution. Fortunately, the 'Red Scare' was short lived, but, unfortunately, it restored the forces of reaction and left devestated civil liberties, the labor movement, and faith in reform. (16)

The founders of the New School believed that new techniques for social change could be fashioned from the social sciences, but they did not translate these beliefs into specific goals for social change. They fashioned the New School as a lecture center to bring about an intellectual transformation, to acquaint the intelligent and educated adult with the latest research and theories from the social sciences. But the founders fashioned no agenda for change, formulated no goals, and organized no programs. They aimed at transforming society by transforming the mind.

The founders could not agree on a program of social research, and they also had become disenchanted with the School as a lecture center. In spite of their reputation as social scientists, many were poor lecturers, notably Thorstein Veblen, and they held the lecture in disrepute. As Johnson noted in his autobiography, 'the intellectuals of that time were very snooty about lectures. Chautauqua and all other lecturing institutions aroused their derision.' (17)

By 1923 the conflict about what the New School should be had been resolved in favor of a general adult education institution, but not without considerable animosity and conflict. So strong had the feelings run that Croly refused to publish Robinson's The Mind in the Making, a book that became a social science classic. (18) The School's administration had fallen into disarray. In reaction to the bureaucratization of Columbia University, Robinson had insisted on an informal administrative structure, but such a structure proved inadequate to the demands for raising funds, securing facilities, staffing lecture courses, and resolving the differences of opinions.

By 1922 it was time to reassess this experiment, for the New School had not achieved its purposes, had split over what the purposes should be, and had financial difficulties. Three Board members asked Alvin Johnson to work out a plan to save the School. Johnson presented two plans to the Board. One was patterned after Croly's desire for a research faculty to work with mature students from the professions and business. The other was patterned after Robinson's idea of a lecture program. The Board accepted the second plan, Croly's faction resigned, and in 1923 Johnson became director of the New School.

With the reorganization in 1923, the short life of the New School as an experiment for social reconstruction ended. With the exception of Alvin Johnson, the founders ceased to play an active role. For some of the founders, such as Dewey, Veblen, and Mitchell, the New School was their one direct venture in adult education. Croly turned from social reform to adult education as a means for cultural regeneration. (19) Beard and Robinson gave leadership to the Workers' Education Bureau, a short-lived project in the 1920s, and to the American Association for Adult Education. Johnson's interest in adult education continued unabated through the New School and the American Association for Adult Education.

CONTRARY AGENDAS FOR ADULT EDUCATION

The differences of opinion about the purpose of the New School foreshadowed differences that would later appear in the larger adult education movement in the twenties and thirties. Some of these contrary agendas for adult education appeared in the differing aspirations that Herbert Croly, James Harvey Robinson, and Alvin Johnson had for the New School.

In The Promise of American Life Croly advanced his thesis of nationalism as the instrument for individual improvement and national development. By tying individual realization to a collective purpose in the nation, Croly believed that a national purpose would create such an invigorating atmosphere that the individual would be liberated. The imperative for a national purpose - a new kind of government and a new kind of citizen - grew out of the economic explosion after the Civil War.

As a consequence of this economic explosion, specialization came to pervade American life. The major specializations - business, politics, and labor - formed specialist organizations, and these organizations in turn fashioned particular intellectual outlooks and manners of life in their members. In their extreme outcomes, these organizations promoted selfish interests.

A healthy society required that persons move beyond selfish interests, beyond individualism, and toward responsibility for the community as a whole. Croly wanted not just social reform, but a reformed society. He wanted to distribute wealth in the national interest, believing that this would advance individual achievement in politics, science, and the arts. If society supported excellence, regenerated men and women would result, and they, in such an atmosphere, would pursue excellence. Croly advocated in his biographer's words, an 'intellectual approach to social problems'. (20) Thinking needed to be reoriented and ideas that were outmoded should be recognized as such and discarded. Croly linked the future of democracy to the dissemination of progressive ideas and information related to political problems. In the words of Levy, his biographer, 'intellectual orientation must precede constructive social change'. (21)

Croly's interest in creating an institution to do social research applied to problems in democracy dated back to 1910 when he advocated a school to train social experts. During the war Croly and Johnson had been impressed by Harold Laski's report of the London School of Economics. Professors there, reportedly, had retained the liberty to address real problems, even if controversial. The London School also trained leaders for the labor movement, which was of particular interest to Croly. But another school - the French Ecole Libre des Sciences Politiques - captured Croly's thinking and became the model upon which he wanted to pattern a new American institution. The Ecole trained public administrators and applied scientific methods to political problems. It also operated independently of state control which gave the faculty independence from interference.

In the New Republic in 1918, Croly outlined his conception of this new American institution, already under discussion. Croly (22) called upon social science to produce 'a technique of social progress'. The industrial revolution and the advent of technology had made research and application of the social sciences imperative. Stimulated by the war, science had become a major resource; however, science wrongly used retarded progress. The 'dominant class', Croly said, had accumulated the 'surplus value' and the power. A 'moral and social particularism' had resulted so that those who gained by science considered the fruit their own. Specialization resulted in technical experts, these experts usually had limited social concerns. Under these conditions, the wholeness of society had been rent and conflict ensued.

Croly envisioned the New School as 'a counter social offensive against the existing kingdoms of scientific particularism and class exclusiveness'. Croly wanted to go beyond the pioneers of the social sciences who sought to identify general laws but did not go on to identify specific social conditions. The sequence Croly wanted proceeded this way:

(a) identify techniques of social progress,
(b) increase the fund of social knowledge, and
(c) validate the social planning that resulted.

In Croly's mind, there was clearly a need for an educational agency to train men and women to 'engineer' social change and for a scientific discipline to study social change. The state and voluntary associations - the present agencies of social experimentation - were not adequate in themselves and no university department produced social engineers. The 'social worker' was the clearest example, but those schools operated from charitable motivations, a narrow focus, and not from scientific impulse. The most pressing need was for 'labor administrators' who would work for methods of co-operation between managers of industry and the rank and file laborers and would reconcile conflicts about productivity standards, houses of labor, employment conditions, and the amount of self-government.

The new social engineers that Croly wanted to train would be competent in two areas. They would be able to organize 'experiments in democratic organization' and to overcome the divorce between ordinary citizens and experts. They would also be competent in the dissemination of ideas. If persons were to learn from experience, knowledge of ideas would have to be propagated. Preparation would include training in the psychology of opinion, how opinions are spread, and how to safeguard the public from methods of propaganda.

Croly's ideas for the New School extended beyond commonly accepted notions of adult education, and they were ultimately rejected by his colleagues in the New School. His ideas about social engineering, practical discipline, and social experimentation belonged more to another tradition of adult education, the tradition notably refined and advanced by Eduard Lindeman, a trusted Croly confidante.

The New School had many founders, but Johnson and Mitchell credit James Harvey Robinson with the idea for the New School and for its guiding philosophy that life and scholarship were interrelated. (23) More than the other founders, Robinson wrestled in two books with the questions of how the adult mind had been made and how the obsolete ideas could be discarded for the newer ideas of the social sciences.

Published in 1921, the first book, The Mind in the Making, addressed the issue of the relation of intelligence to social reform. Written while Robinson was at the New School and when Wilson was nearing the end of his term and the beginning of Harding's 'return to normalcy', the book provides an example of the 'New History' at work, explicates a theory of cultural transmission, and critiques the then current philosophy of repression.

History, Robinson said, can assist in understanding the present predicament through studying how man came to think as he did. History that increased intelligence studied the past with an eye on the present. History pointed out the conditions under which beliefs still held in the present were formulated. Beliefs about human nature and social organizations were formed in response to specific environmental conditions. But most persons, Robinson charged, were too preoccupied with everyday matters to reflect on their beliefs. When their beliefs were challenged they merely rationalized the usefulness of their beliefs. History also challenged the belief of continuity between present beliefs and past beliefs. In fact, there was discontinuity, and the best example was how business had come to dominate American life. The present society so focused on material acquisition that to question business practices was the same as challenging patriotism or religion.

Knowledge in society was advanced by only a few people whom Robinson called 'seers': persons able to escape from 'the sanctified blindness of their time'. The heroes for Robinson were the natural scientists who, standing against the medieval church and its authoritative pronouncements, evolved new and more adequate explanations. Scientific knowledge had affected life mostly through application, through technology, but the changes wrought by these technologies had not been accompanied by changes in the understanding of human nature and social relationships. That was the task of social science, but the present climate opposed examining social beliefs and behavior.

The philosophy of repression that now prevailed sought to safeguard American society from any foreign ideas, casting suspicion on even those like Robinson who suggested open-mindedness.

Robinson advocated no reform platform; he did not suggest any ways that the social order should be reconstructed. His only agenda for reform was to call for the release of intelligence, the production and application of knowledge to the study of man and society. His agenda was to bring the mind up to date. Schools and universities had already proven they could not perform this function of criticism of practices in the economic, political, religious, and social institutions. The New School, in contrast, provided opportunity for this kind of continued learning.

After his resignation from the New School, Robinson turned his attention to popularizing the new knowledge. Beginning in 1922 he edited a series of books for the Workers' Education Bureau of New York City. Called The Workers' Bookshelf, the books sought to popularize the new scientific knowledge. One of these, Robinson's The Humanizing of Knowledge, proposed a means for the dissemination of knowledge. (24) In this short book published in 1924 Robinson anticipated the adult education agenda for 30 years. Robinson restated his position in The Mind in the Making that scientific knowledge had not been widely disseminated or accepted. Most people regarded the scientific attitude of mind with hostility and did not believe that it should be applied to traditional ideas about the family, property, morality, or the state.

To reach the public with the new knowledge would require a new class of writers and teachers dedicated to the deliberate diffusion of knowledge. They should be researchers themselves who were continuing their research to discover new patterns of known knowledge. Effective disseminators would strip knowledge of its professional character and become 're-assorters, selectors, combiners, and illuminators' for the general public.

Reaching the general reader required the creation of a new literary form, books were not then written for the general reader. Books written for the general reader should first enlist the reader's attention, then present the information so the general reader could understand and fit it into his life, and finally suggest the significance of the information to the reader. In length, the new literary form should be between a book and a journal article. The aim would be to bring together information on a topic to excite the reader so his ideas and outlook could be broadened and changed but not to present the 'principles' or 'outline' of a recognized science.

Knowledge had become fragmented, divided into specializations. Divisions of knowledge - essential in research - raised barriers that made teachers ineffective in the education of the young and the public at large. Scholars and students alike were left without an integrated view of knowledge and its relation to life. All knowledge, Robinson believed, was interdependent. Knowledge of man and his world had to be resynthesized; otherwise, knowledge was useless. In this regard, scholarly persons were just as 'uneducated' as laymen. The specialists knew one segment of knowledge but were unaware of the other areas.

If the task of humanizing knowledge required a new type of writers, teachers, and literary form, it also required new agencies. The institutions of learning - at the public school and university level - were so entrenched with their vested interests and routines as to be useless in this endeavor. Robinson found in adult education the possibility of a humanizing agency. In the United States, new agencies had appeared, including the New School, the Workers' Education Bureau, labor colleges, and study circles.

When Alvin Johnson became director in 1923, he set a new agenda in motion. For four years - 1919-1923 - the New School had pioneered a model of the university - freed from restraint and bureaucratization - as an agency of adult education. But Robinson's dream of the New School as a gentleman's club for intellectual endeavors ignored administrative and economic realities. Johnson found no fault with Robinson's ideas about a lecture program. He had disagreed with Croly's notion of a school for social change, but he had not objected. Without compromising his beliefs, he had avoided making enemies of the two factions.

What he apparently wanted from the beginning was 'a true school of adult education', a school to continue the education of the already educated. (27) Providing education for workers without a high school education was remedial education that belonged to the public school system. The educated bore heavy social responsibility and their mind needed to 'remain clear and steady'. Unfortunately, the educated mind tended to accept quickly the dominant opinions of the time. In the war the ceaseless promotion of slogans to establish certain attitudes had permeated even the educated minds.

Johnson's interest in adult education had found expression immediately after he received his doctorate in 1901. In 1902, the very next year, he embarked upon two projects that embodied the concerns that occupied him for the remainder of his life. One concern was the integration of the social sciences for realistic application to practical problems. In 1902 he was invited to write articles and to be the economics editor for the New International Encyclopaedia, edited by Frank Moore Colby. Part of his reason for taking the job was to immerse himself in the whole range of the social sciences. He had concluded that the 'social sciences needed to be integrated if they were to deal with practical problems realistically.' (26) The second was how to interpret the social sciences to adult laypersons. An invitation in 1902 by a correspondence school to write a textbook on economics that adult laymen could understand without a teacher introduced Johnson to adult education. The school folded, but his book was sold to D.C. Heath & Company and published.

By 1912 the year that Johnson began his professorship at Cornell, he had become convinced that the economic sciences could not be understood by intelligent laymen. As he said, 'The divorce between academic economics and the intelligent public was nearly complete'. (27) College alumni did not remember the economic theory they had learned in college. If economics was to contribute to public opinion and public policy, it had to reach the lay public. Believing that this connection could be made by writing, Johnson wrote an article for the Atlantic Monthly, which was published. He was invited to write more. At Cornell he continued to practice writing for the intelligent layman.

The principal community agency for disseminating scholarly and literary works to the lay public was the library. At the invitation of Henry S. Pritchett, President of the Carnegie Corporation in 1914, Johnson conducted a ten-week tour to inspect the Carnegie built libraries. His report contained a mixed review, citing many inaccessible poorly managed libraries with few books. He also found some dedicated librarians who kept informed about community events and informed community members of relevant books. He called the libraries 'the Cinderellas of the educational world, with no prince upon the horizon'. (28)

When Johnson left Cornell to join the New Republic staff, he did not plan to abandon academic life. But he saw his editorial work as a form of education, as a way of getting near the lay public. It served as a bridge to close the gap between the academic specialist and the general public. Johnson had found his vocation as a generalist, refusing as Max Lerner said, to be circumscribed by any specialities, using the specialities instead 'as a window on the world'. (29)

Upon becoming Director in 1923, Johnson changed the direction of the New School toward adult education. The New School became a lecture center, using non-faculty as instructors, catering to students as consumers, and involving them in administration. The curriculum expanded to include vocational programs and the arts. Johnson created a research school in the thirties with faculty exiles from Germany and later organized a graduate school and undergraduate degree programs. The New School still flourishes.

NOTES

1.　Carol S. Gruber, Mars and Minerva: World War I and the Uses of the Higher Learning in America, (Louisiana State University Press, Baton Rouge, LA, 1975), p.7.
2.　Ibid., pp.14-15.
3.　Edward T. Silva and Sheila Slaughter, Serving Power: The Making of the Academic Social Science Expert, (Greenwood Press, Westport, CT, 1984), pp.13-16.
4.　Gruber, Mars and Minerva, p.9.
5.　Ibid., p.5.
6.　Richard Hofstadter, The Progressive Historians: Turner, Beard, Parrington (Vintage Books, NY, 1970), pp.181-6.

7.   Morton White, Social Thought in America: The Revolt Against Formalism, (Beacon, Boston, 1949).

8.   Ibid., p.12.

9.   Hosdtadter, Progressive Historians, p.185.

10.   From the considerable literature on the founders of the New School, I made extensive use of the following: John Braeman, 'What is the Good of History? The Case of James Harvey Robinson', Amerikastudien, 30, 1 (1985), pp.75-89; Alvin Johnson, Pioneer's Progress: An Autobiography, (University of Nebraska Press, 1960; org. publ. Viking Press, NY, 1952); David W. Levy, Herbert Croly of the New Republic: The Life and Thought of an American Progressive, (Princeton University Press, Princeton, NJ, 1985), 335 pp.; Lucy Sprague Mitchell, Two Lives: The Story of Wesley Clair Mitchell and Myself, (Simon and Schuster, NY, 1953); Ellen Nore, Charles A. Beard: An Intellectual Biography, (Illinois University Press, Carbondale, IL, 1983), pp.87-95, Peter M. Rutkoff and William B. Scott, New School: A History of the New School for Social Research, (Free Press, NY, 1986).

11.   Levy, Herbert Croly, p.95.

12.   Johnson, Pioneer's Progress, pp.271-88.

13.   James Harvey Robinson, 'The New School', School and Society, 11, (January 31, 1920), pp.129-32.

14.   Mitchell, Two Lives, p.339.

15.   Rutkoff and Scott, New School, p.20.

16.   Robert K. Murray, Red Scare: A Study in National Hysteria, 1919-1920, (McGraw-Hill, NY, 1964), pp.17, 170, 176-7.

17.   Johnson, Pioneer's Progress, p.279.

18.   James Harvey Robinson, The Mind in the Making: The Relation of Intelligence to Social Reform, (Harper and Brothers, NY, 1921).

19.   Herbert Croly, 'Education for Grown-Ups', New Republic, 37, (December 12, 1923), pp.59-61.

20.   David Levy, Herbert Croly, p.142.

21.   Ibid.

22.   Herbert Croly, 'A School of Social Research', New Republic, 15, (June 8, 1918), pp.167-71.

23.   Johnson, Pioneer's Progress, p.235; Mitchell, Two Lives, pp.333-4.

24.   James Harvey Robinson, The Humanizing of Knowledge, (George H. Doran Company, NY, 1924).

25.   Johnson, Pioneer's Progress, p.273.

26.   Ibid., p.158.

27.   Ibid., pp.225-6.
28.   Ibid., p.237.
29.   Max   Lerner,   'Foreword',   in   Alvin   Johnson,
Pioneer's Progress, (University of Nebraska, Lincoln, NB,
1960, 1952), pp. ix-xvi.

Chapter Two

THE CARNEGIE CORPORATION, THE AMERICAN ASSOCIATION FOR ADULT EDUCATION, AND THE PROMOTION OF AN IDEA OF ADULT EDUCATION

In the interwar period, from 1924 to 1941, the most active force in the adult education field was not an adult education institution or scholar but a philanthropic foundation: the Carnegie Corporation of New York City. To achieve its goals in adult education, the Corporation organized and used the American Association for Adult Education (AAAE). The Carnegie Corporation's activity in adult education was an experiment to promote a particular idea of adult education and to foster its acceptance among the organizations that claimed to have adult education as their major interest. This experiment remains without precedence in American history. Neither before nor since has a foundation through its philanthropic activities or any national agency - public or private - sought in such a thorough fashion to impose a unifying principle on the various segments of the field of adult education.

ORGANIZING TO ADVANCE THE IDEA OF ADULT EDUCATION

Early historians of adult education such as C. Hartley Grattan (1) and Malcolm Knowles (2) attributed the Carnegie Corporation's support of adult education to the interest of Frederick P. Keppel (1875-1943) whose term as President from 1923-41 spanned the Carnegie years of support, 1924-41. In reality, the Carnegie support for adult education grew out of efforts to define the foundation's role in the advancement and diffusion of knowledge, an effort underway before Keppel's presidency. Keppel neither 'discovered' adult education nor had to persuade the Board of Trustees to support it. (3)

When Keppel became President, his predecessors and the Board of Trustees had already chartered a direction and established policies for the granting of foundation monies. The principal architects of this policy were Elihu Root of the Carnegie Corporation, James R. Angell who served as President for 1920-21, and Henry Pritchett, President of the Carnegie Foundation for the Advancement of Teaching since 1905, and acting President of the Carnegie Corporation from Angell's resignation until Keppel's appointment.

Andrew Carnegie founded the Carnegie Corporation of New York in 1911 as an agency for his philanthropic activities and directed its work for the first few years. He died in 1919. Carnegie had believed that his donations should be in those areas where knowledge might best be advanced and where knowledge could be made accessible to the largest number of people. Though he based his gifts on values - mainly middle-class virtues of honesty, thrift, and morality - he refused to define what knowledge should be diffused.

Root and Pritchett disagreed. They believed that there were pressing national problems toward which knowledge should be directed. Diffusing general knowledge for individual enlightenment to the largest number of individuals was an inadequate response. Instead, 'experts' should select the knowledge to be diffused to the 'people'. Such a position required the officers and Board of Trustees of the Corporation to select their own priorities rather than simply responding to requests brought to them for funding.

In this decision, Lagemann said, the Carnegie Corporation aligned itself with the new public policy of the twentieth century: expert decision-making combined with expert knowledge and widest dissemination of this expertise to the public. (4) The Corporation implemented this policy with grants to such agencies as the National Academy of Science, the National Research Council, and the Social Science Research Council. Two commissioned studies related directly to adult education.

In 1918 the Carnegie Corporation commissioned ten books in a series called Americanization Studies: The Acculturation of Immigrant Groups into American Society. The purpose was not to critique the Americanization movement from a policy perspective but to find out how the foreign born had been transformed into Americans, how the process actually worked, and what institutions in American life had been involved. Ten areas of study were chosen to focus on specific institutions or complex of social forces. (5)

Frank V. Thompson, Assistant Superintendent of Schools in Boston, wrote the first book in the series, Schooling of the Immigrant. (6) He regarded the education of the immigrant as part of the larger problem of education for citizenship of all Americans and as the responsibility of many institutions, not only the schools. The problem of teaching adult immigrants was part of the larger problem of teaching adults as contrasted to teaching immature children. Thompson believed successful teaching with adults should take the form of a friendly service given by one person to another who respect one another to achieve a common purpose and which gives the student examples of what to do. Thompson called this the 'educational service stations' approach. (7)

While Acting President of the Corporation from 1921-23, Henry Pritchett brought William S. Learned from the Carnegie Foundation to assist him in formulating policy and, in particular, to study library problems. Learned reported his investigation in a memorandum which Keppel had published in 1924 as The American Public Library and the Diffusion of Knowledge. (8) Learned called for the public library to become the 'community intelligence center' in which trained personnel would make available books on specific subjects related to the specific needs and interests of adults in the community.

Behind this recommendation lay an insightful analysis of the problem of knowledge diffusion and adult education. The opportunity that presented itself to the Carnegie Corporation in the twenties, as Learned saw it, appeared like this. The diffusion of knowledge should no longer be left to chance, that is, left to individuals to pick and choose what they wanted to learn. The amount and complexity of information had greatly increased. Wider areas of human experience had become the objects of scientific inquiry, and newer and faster means of communication had increased the speed for disseminating knowledge. Those who undertook this task should not expect success to come quickly or easily, and they should not regard it as a neutral activity. Those who received new ideas changed their conduct and sometimes in a direction not desired by those who had spread the ideas.

New methods to make knowledge available for general

use would have to be developed through experimentation. The experimentation should be based on one fundamental principle: knowledge should be adapted to make the information appropriate to the recipients and their needs. Learned believed that the conditions were present for successful experimentation. The increased success of the public schools in diffusing knowledge demonstrated that any body of knowledge could be taught to anyone if organized and taught at their level of ability. The public school success had been contingent, first, on the development of instruments to identify, measure, and classify the traits and mental abilities of the students, and, secondly, on the adaptation of the materials - through experimentation and testing - to the various combinations of abilities of the students.

Most of the elements necessary to successful diffusion were already in place: adult education activities, adult motives for applying knowledge, adults with leisure time, and communities capable of organizing for action. But ideas and leadership were lacking. The many educational activities on behalf of adults had not been undergirded by systematic study of how adults went about learning in their daily lives and how their attention could be directed to materials in print addressed to their concerns. Learned called this 'putting the community to school', but the principles of this educational service for adults had not yet been identified. (9)

The Corporation's Board directed Frederick Keppel to initiate a program of adult education - to be directed toward service goals and not profit goals - in anticipation of increased leisure time and the need for out-of-school educational opportunities. To implement this policy, Keppel convened a panel of experts in 1924 to advise the Corporation on a possible role in adult education. Following their generally favorable response, the Corporation then convened regional conferences to explore the need for a national organization and commissioned a series of studies about various aspects of adult education. Two years later, in 1926, these activities culminated in the organization of the American Association for Adult Education.

For whatever his reasons, Keppel chose to implement the Carnegie program of adult education through studies, research, demonstrations, and experiments. In this decision, Keppel, in several respects, ignored the recommendations he had received. Learned, for example, had recommended making the library - present in almost every community - into the 'community intelligence center'. But the recommendation to create a new institutional form for the diffusion of knowledge to the adult population was ignored. Furthermore, Eduard C. Lindeman, a member of the advisory panel Keppel had assembled, recommended studying adult education as a social movement: examine the social conditions to which adult education institutions and programs were responses. Instead, the studies of adult education centred on institutional delivery systems and not on the social and organizational dynamics of adult education as a new educational innovation.

Instead of choosing as Executive-Director a person who had distinguished himself in one area of adult education, the Executive Board of the newly formed Association, as if to cement its relationship with the Carnegie Corporation, chose as the Executive-Director, Morse A. Cartwright (1890-1974), Keppel's administrative assistant. Cartwright had come to the Carnegie Corporation in 1924 from the University of California at Berkeley, where he had held several administrative positions. His only experience in adult education had been his brief tenure as the assistant director of the university's extension division.

INTERPRETING THE IDEA OF ADULT EDUCATION

A policy pronounced was not necessarily the same as the policy implemented. The Carnegie experiment through the AAAE became one not of the diffusion of knowledge but of the diffusion of a particular conception of adult education, namely, liberal education. The principles for organizing and applying knowledge to individual and social needs were derived from the purposes of liberal education: to create open-mindedness and tolerance. Frederick Keppel, Morse Cartwright, and Dorothy Canfield Fisher were the principal interpreters of the Carnegie position.

As President of the Carnegie Corporation, Frederick Keppel made few public statements about adult education. But on two occasions in 1926, in a Yale Review article and a speech at the Chautauqua Institution, he made his most comprehensive statement about adult education. (10) As Keppel saw it, adult education had grown up without direction from organized education and without guidance and control from any source. Using a military metaphor,

Keppel described the regular educational system - public schools and colleges - as an army, well staffed and organized. But the educational militia - those for whom education was a part-time activity - was almost neglected by educators.

Adult education that encompassed all the educational needs of adults could not be narrowly defined. Rather, Keppel regarded adult education as 'the process of learning, on the initiative of the individual, seriously and consecutively undertaken as a supplement to some primary occupation'. (11) Such learning could take place at anytime after a person's individual schooling had ended. And it could begin at any place on the educational ladder, ranging from remedial education to classes for physicians or engineering executives. Keppel wanted education to be 'a continuing process' that was not haphazard in adulthood.

Keppel wanted to enlarge the purposes that adult education programs served. Most adult education could be classified as vocational or as part of the propaganda efforts of an organization, what Keppel called 'pointed education'. Opportunities for consecutive study in subjects such as history, literature, science and the fine arts were lacking. Adults needed to study these subjects, not as an academic process, but to improve their lives and the general state of culture in America. Keppel regarded adult education as 'an agency of very definite importance in making life better worth living for the American citizen'. (12) In 1926, he had high hopes that such adult education programs would solve the problems of persons who did not know what to do with their new leisure, of the unhappy and maladjusted - as indicated by the high incidence of suicides and criminal behavior - and of persons stampeded in many directions by new ideas because they lacked the knowledge and truths which they could learn from the experience of mankind.

Keppel also wanted to make certain aspects of the adult education operation more efficient. Most adults stopped their education when they completed the formal educational requirements, and for those who did continue there was usually a lag of several years between school completion and entrance into adult education. Educators in the formal educational system, including high schools, colleges, and professionals school, did not recognize the importance of continuing learning nor did they prepare students to continue their own learning. (13) But for learning to be a continuing process students needed not only desire but also information about how they could continue their learning. As Keppel put it, educators in the formal educational system should prepare students for education as a secondary occupation.

Educators of adults faced the unique problem of having to get the interest of adults and relating materials to their problems and everyday concerns. Keppel wanted research to measure the educational capacities of adults and to modify college testing programs for adults. Given the pervasiveness of commercial adult education agencies, a program for adults to test their own capacities to benefit would prevent dropouts and wasted time and money.

To Morse A. Cartwright, the Executive-Director of the AAAE from its inception in 1926 to 1949, fell the major responsibility for interpreting the Carnegie idea, a task which he performed faithfully and articulately. The first step, oddly enough, was to avoid having to define, in any explicit way, what the Corporation meant by adult education. Participants at the Carnegie Corporation sponsored Cleveland Conference in 1925 were persuaded not to make 'either an exclusive or an inclusive definition of adult education'. (14) Conference participants decided to permit 'American adult education to define itself'.

In reality, the AAAE did espouse a position. As Cartwright so diplomatically described it: adult education as an idea could not be identified with immigrant education, workers' education, university extension, or with any aspect that 'did not make directly for a safe, sane and careful upbuilding of the central idea of adult education as a continuing cultural process pursued without ulterior purpose'. (15) The AAAE refused to define or endorse a definition of adult education because, in Cartwright's assessment, it was too early to tell what the term 'adult education' might come to mean in the United States. Cartwright contended that the AAAE maintained a middle of the road approach, for identifying with one aspect of adult education would have also meant identifying with a particular economic, religious or moral position.

Initially, AAAE emphasized cultural studies to the exclusion of vocational studies, but by 1930 the Association had tempered that decision. Cartwright claimed in his Annual Report of 1931-32 that the Association did not need to take a definite stand because the two positions could be reconciled.

Cartwright could avoid defining adult education, but he

could not avoid describing it. In his annual reports, articles, and speeches, Cartwright resorted to slogans, calling adult education 'a lifelong process', 'continuing growth throughout life rather than a mere preparation for living', and 'a lifelong expanding process of enrichment in moral and spiritual, as well as in vocational, values'. And in his ten-year assessment of the Carnegie experiment, Cartwright argued that the idea of schooling as a 'preparation for life' had to be abandoned in favor of the idea of 'live and learn'. (16) The idea of education as a process of 'live and learn' constituted a new educational policy in which education was related closely to the daily lives of the people.

In describing the purposes of adult education, Cartwright echoed what Keppel had said earlier. Adult education widely diffused throughout the country would offset undesirable traits in American culture: its utilitarian and materialistic values. The Association wanted to develop in the United States a culture that would enrich the life of individuals and deepen the content of national life. (17)

To popularize the technical reports published as books in 1926 as part of a Studies in Adult Education series, the AAAE asked Dorothy Canfield Fisher to write a book for the general American public. (18) Published in 1927 as Why Stop Learning?, the Carnegie Corporation made a grant of $3,600 to the AAAE to distribute it in Europe and the United States. Cartwright called it 'the adult education publication of the year'. (19)

The AAAE often used for its project persons who were well-known to the public. Fisher, a novelist and short story writer, also wrote non-fiction. When the Book-of-the-Month was organized in 1926, Fisher became a member of the Board of Judges. Rubin (20) characterized her as almost anti-modern in temperament, concerned about the dominance of business values, the decline of cultural standards, and the preservation of democracy. Fisher claimed that she wrote Why Stop Learning? from the perspective of an intelligent citizen, but she was far from the average lay person for whom she wrote.

Fisher's belief that the war had revealed the precariousness of democracy underscored, for her as it did for others, the importance of adult education to equip adults for a world growing increasingly more complex and devoid of meaning. The next campaign of democracy would be over 'the possibility and advisibility of general education' for adults, just as the battle of the nineteenth century had been

29

over the education of children. (21)

Battle lines in adult education had already been drawn, Fisher believed, over the issues of what constituted the cultured person and whether culture should be accessible to everyone. Conservatives believed that the great masses of the American people were inferior to them and should not be given access to the cultural objects which they possessed. Advocates of adult education for everyone had not helped their case by claiming that persons could become informed and cultivated by reading a five-foot shelf of books, by equating the acquisition of information with education, or by claiming that getting education would result in making more money.

Other problems, Fisher also noted, confronted the new movement: complexity of life in the twenties, increased leisure, and loss of meaning. Adults could not cope with this complexity without the kind of education that helped them acquire intelligence and broadmindedness; education was not merely the acquisition of information. Leisure had been thrust upon persons unprepared to use it, and they were left with 'a new bleak emptiness', a force that drove them to education or after more excitement, sports, entertainment, and material possessions. Adults were also experiencing another condition of modern life: the absence of any general motive for living. In an earlier period religious beliefs had provided for many persons that motive, but a new, more humanistic faith in the better qualities of humanity which should be cherished and nurtured had not yet fully emerged. (22)

DEFENDING THE IDEA OF ADULT EDUCATION

In the twenties, stable political and economic circumstances favored the Carnegie experiment in adult education for cultural enrichment. But these favourable circumstances suddenly and irrevocably changed with the economic depression and emergence of totalitarian governments in Europe. The stock market crash October, 1929, heralded, Cartwright believed, 'America's coming of age in both an economic and intellectual sense'. (23) Those who had been caught in this economic debacle had raised questions about social and governmental institutions. Educational groups had become aware of the extent to which economics was a powerful force in ordinary life activities, and some educators argued that if the economic system was wrong, then it should be changed. The education system should be changed as well to make the school an agency of social change.

This emphasis on social action roused Cartwright's ire. In his annual reports, he took dead aim at the advocates of adult education for social change. In doing so, he made explicit the Carnegie social philosophy that had been hidden by the experimental nature of the AAAE's work.

Cartwright understood this interest in social change. In a brief but perceptive section in his 1933-34 annual report, Cartwright showed how closely the dominant interests of particular ages were intertwined with the form that adult education took. Because of the interest in the social sciences, it was natural that persons took interest in social change. Educators at all levels of the educational ladder - including adult educators - considered the objectives of education from the perspective of social change. Many educators regarded social reorganization as an educational problem for the adult generation. (24) Cartwright accused them of making 'education' and 'propaganda' synonymous.

Cartwright could not support social change as a policy for adult education or for any level of education. He proclaimed himself an educational liberal who sought to promote open-mindedness as the goal of adult education. As an educational liberal he stood between the conservatives and the 'radical extremists', as he called them. He could not agree with the conservatives who had no skepticism about the present economic and social situation and who fought to keep things as they were. Nor could he agree with the radical liberals who had, to him, deserted the philosophy of open-mindedness in education to work for popular causes and profound social change. So extreme was their position to Cartwright that he described them as communists or fascists in their views. (25)

Schools and adult education agencies prepared people for social action through open-minded investigation of various sides of issues but not through 'emotionalizing' the content of education. (26) The Carnegie Corporation sponsored Des Moines Forum programs, directed by John Studebaker, which exemplified Cartwright's open-minded approach. The forums presented different points of view, not to stimulate action, but to promote understanding. (27)

Those who wanted to use education to promote specific social changes had overestimated the power of education.

(28) The social order developed out of economic and spiritual values. Cartwright was not disturbed that education lagged behind economic, social, and political thinking. Indeed, educational thinking should lag behind economic thinking. If education was to be integrated into 'the business of living', then the economic basis upon which one's living depended must be determined first. Only then could planners proceed safely with creating an education system. A new educational system - including adult education - would require experimentation, research and demonstration projects, but these should not be conducted as part of a predetermined scheme of education.

These social and economic ideas were not just evoked by the special circumstances of the thirties. The adult education movement in the United States after World War I was built on the traditional American assumption of the classless society. Labor was regarded as a function, not a class, and education for the workers was education for a function, not education for living in a particular social class. Cartwright (29) argued in his ten-year report that the United States had no class of people denied educational opportunity though some persons were educationally underprivileged. Cartwright saw no educational wrong to right or a need to provide for the underprivileged something they had been denied. The need was to provide 'an ideal of continuous education throughout life for all types of adult individuals'. (30)

Looking at the adult education movement retrospectively in 1940, Alvin Johnson, President of the New School for Social Research and an active participant in the AAAE, identified four assumptions upon which the leaders of the adult education movement based their decisions. (31) They regarded all classes as inadequately equipped to deal with the new problems and the emerging social and political issues of the time. They believed that the rapid advance of technology would result in national prosperity for all and in leisure for wide masses of the people to enjoy music, art, reading, and other cultural activities. They recognized that the rapid economic revolution would make some occupations and skills obsolete and that displaced workers would need intellectual flexibility to learn new work skills. They believed that a world economically enriched could offer better treatment to the handicapped and make life more tolerable for them.

Leaders of the adult education movement, Johnson said,

did not regard these problems as class problems nor believe that class education could solve them. In keeping with the spirit of American democracy, they wanted to avoid narrowly focusing adult education. It should, instead, be broadly focused and appeal to all classes.

IMPLEMENTING THE ADULT EDUCATION IDEA

Whatever the AAAE may have been to its members and the organizations with which it worked, the AAAE was to the Carnegie Corporation an experimental project. The Carnegie Corporation used the AAAE's Executive Board as its 'grants review board' to approve grants for adult education projects. The Corporation also provided the AAAE's operating funds through grants, and the leaders of the AAAE, beyond assesssing modest membership fees, made no attempt to become financially independent. By 1936 the Carnegie Corporation had invested four and a half million dollars in adult education, nearly three and a half million of this sum through the association. (32) The grants supported projects that reached into almost every area of adult education in American life. This attempt to impose an idea of adult education - a social policy - upon the United States followed three principal strategies.

The first strategy was to provide a scientific basis for an adult psychology and pedagogy. In the first year or two of Keppel's presidency, the Carnegie Corporation commissioned Edward L. Thorndike to conduct a study of the learning ability of adults and later a study of adult interests, which were published as Adult Learning in 1928 and as Adult Interests in 1935. (33) Keppel's choice of Thorndike was not by chance, for he and Thorndike were close personal friends and the Carnegie Corporation supported Thorndike's Division of Educational Psychology at Teachers College Institute of Educational Research.

In brief, Thorndike found that adults between 20 and 50 maintained, with some slight decrease, their ability to learn. What Thorndike described as learning ability was really learning efficiency: how much information an adult could learn in what length of time. The study of adult interests found that adults retained interests which they had in their twenties into the later stages of life.

Cartwright called Thorndike's research on adult learning 'the most important factor in the spread of the adult education idea in the last decade'. (34) In particular, this research supported two major ideas. First, education did not have to be confined to the schooling of children and youth because adults could learn, too. No longer would schools have to provide enough information to last a lifetime. Such research should alter the structure of American education, a process that Cartwright predicted would occur in one to two decades (35). Second, the research on adult interests supported the Carnegie idea that participation in adult education should be voluntary and not compulsory. Because the interests of adults did not diminish as they got older, they would engage in adult education voluntarily to pursue their interests.

On a first reading, most persons probably joined Cartwright in praising Thorndike's contribution, but a closer examination by discerning readers would also have shown that Thorndike intended his findings to be used - as all science ultimately aims to do - to predict and control. Thorndike was not an educational equalitarian. He shared the same hereditarian view of intelligence that guided the work of the psychologists who constructed and administered the Army Alpha Beta tests. (36) They believed, as did Thorndike, that persons were not equally endowed with intelligence and that intelligence tests should be used to identify levels of intelligence for school and vocational placement. Thorndike included his social philosophy views in both reports. He advocated testing to screen for those adults who were most able to benefit from adult education; resources then should be directed toward these. Similarly, the interests of adults could be used to determine how and to whom adult education opportunities should be distributed.

Closely related research studies were conducted on adult reading. The most notable were <u>Reading Interests and Habits of Adults</u> by W.S. Gray and Ruth Munroe (37) and <u>What People Want to Read About</u> by Douglas Waples and Ralph Tyler. (38) Waples and Tyler developed an instrument to identify the interest of adults so that libraries would have some indication of what adults wanted to learn. In a Carnegie funded project, the national YMCA adapted the Waples and Tyler instrument to use as an 'interest finder' to survey the adults of a small community, Meriden, Connecticut. (39)

A second strategy was to make the liberal idea of adult education the normative idea by which the work of all segments of the field would be judged. The most important of these Carnegie Corporation commissioned studies explored prisoner education, adult education for blacks, rural adult education, and science as a subject matter for adults. (40) The authors of these studies referred in their reports to previous Carnegie studies and to adult education abroad. They had thoroughly surveyed the status of adult education in their particular segment, critiqued the form and organization from the liberal perspective, and recommended a reformulation of goals and procedures in light of the liberal approach. In essence, they imposed a normative definition of adult education upon the focused work of these segments. In some segments, adult educators were able to use such a normative idea to improve the quality and scope of educational offerings. With other special populations such as blacks the liberal idea served to obscure the harmful economic and political consequences of segregation.

A third strategy was to promote organizations to support and co-ordinate the work of institutions already engaged in adult education, through what Ralph Beals called the associated leadership approach. (40) The Carnegie Corporation did not create new, permanent agencies of adult education as, for example, the founders of the New School for Social Research had done. Grants from the Carnegie Corporation through the AAAE went to provide temporary support for existing agencies or to create new co-ordinating agencies.

To implement the idea of adult education through existing institutions, the Corporation financed studies on community educational needs and community council programs in urban areas, rural areas, small towns, and suburban communities. The Corporation also supported the first state association, the California Association for Adult Education, which promoted programs statewide. The Des Moines, Iowa, Public School community-wide forum program initiated a new approach: one agency in the community provides a program for all persons in the community and not just for members or clients of their agency. The AAAE through Carnegie grants helped organize the National Advisory Council on Radio in Education, the National Occupational Conference, the Adjustment Service of New York, and the New York Adult Education Council.

Keppel recognized the importance of 'service stations' or middle men in education and cultural activities. (42) Service stations - professional associations, the Department of Agriculture through state extension services, foundations, and ad hoc agencies such as the Anti-Tuberculosis Agency - provided services for members, communities, and agencies. Some service agencies were hard to maintain because there was permanent need but no single profession to support it. The AAAE was an example of this kind of service agency.

The issue of community co-ordination was never settled, but in a speech before the 1935 annual conference of the National University Extension Association, Ralph Beals, an AAAE staff member, made clear the Carnegie position in support of an associated leadership approach versus 'a nationally integrated program of adult education'. Only the federal government had the resources to support a nationally integrated program, but the division between the federal-state responsibilities made such a program almost impossible. Nor did it appear likely that a non-governmental agency such as the AAAE or one of the 400 or so organizations that claimed to devote most of their money and energy to adult education could provide direction for a program national in scope.

For a time in the thirties it appeared that the federal government emergency relief program would pose a threat to the associated leadership approach. Several programs through the Works Progress Administration, in particular, put unemployed teachers to work teaching adults. A panel on emergency education at the 1936 AAAE conference noted several problems with federal involvement. These programs placed control at the wrong level of government - the federal and state level - and not the community level. Government planning for adult education had increased the interest in turning the liberal approach to adult education into social action and propaganda. (43)

Cartwright feared that these emergency education efforts had placed adult education in danger of becoming an instrument of special interests. By 1939 Cartwright described a trend toward increased tolerance in American society during the past twelve to 15 years. He attributed the increased tolerance, as he perceived it, to adult education in general and to two aspects of adult education in particular: the liberal education approach and the 'machinery' of adult education. In its organization, adult education was unregimented, carried on by numberless, uncontrolled bodies, unattached to any single concept or group of concepts. These bodies were not dependent on government grants, but even tax-supported programs enjoyed great autonomy at the local level. Because adult education - considered collectively - had many forms and was highly diversified, there was room for adherents of many diverse opinions. Cartwright regarded this diversity as a strength. (44)

ASSESSING THE RESULTS OF THE CARNEGIE EXPERIMENT

On 19 May, 1941, the Secretary of the Carnegie Corporation notified the officers and the executive board of the AAAE that support would not continue beyond 30 September, 1941. Well before this notification the AAAE had ceased its experimental work and had begun to assess its achievements. In his 1935-36 annual report, Cartwright asked again about whether the association should continue. For ten years the association had supported the idea of adult education. It had made 'constructive criticism' of the adult education movement but had refused to prescribe standards of excellence or to be a publicity agency supporting all types of adult education.

Cartwright believed that the idea of adult education was well established among the organizations involved in any substantial way with adult education. The task before the association now, if it were to continue, was to maintain the ideals of adult education: improve methods and emphasize standards and qualitative performance as the only tests of validity. The association, Cartwright claimed, was now the custodian of 'a body of doctrine' formed from the various experiments and studies of the past ten years. During the next five years (the terms of the Carnegie grant), the association should determine, Cartwright said, whether its role in adult education should continue or should be assumed by another organization.

Beginning in 1936 the AAAE commissioned a series of studies under the title of Social Significance of Adult Education to assess the results of this experiment. In all, 27 books - mainly, short descriptive studies of greatly uneven quality - were published in the series. The most critical discussion of the idea of adult education, however, took place in the pages of the AAAE's Journal of Adult Education. Mary L. Ely put the best of these pieces in Adult Education in Action, (1936); in his foreward, Charles A. Beard called the selections 'original documents' of diversity of ideas about adult education as a movement.

The contributors - educators, intellectuals, and civic leaders - were far from agreed about what this movement should be about and what it had accomplished. Opinions about the purposes ranged from the cultural, to diffusing knowledge, and to preparing adults for new occupations. Some believed that the adult education movement had succeeded in elevating the cultural and knowledge level of the adult public. This success had come about because adult education opportunities had been widely distributed through many agencies.

Others dissented. Changes in cultural taste and knowledge could only be achieved by teaching specific information, not just by making the opportunity widely available. Education made available to adults could not, by itself, foster change. What could be accomplished through adult education depended on the abilities of adults who came into the programs. The key institution for producing adults who had ability to learn was the public education system.

Cartwright's claims about the success of the Carnegie experiment were to be expected. But the achievements of the Carnegie experiment in adult education have yet to be critically assessed. Not the least of the achievements was the body of literature which resulted from the Carnegie funded projects, a literature as yet unanalyzed and unassimilated into the literature of adult education.

NOTES

1.   C. Hartley Grattan, In Quest of Knowledge: A Historical Perspective on Adult Education, (Arno Press and The New York Times, New York, 1971).

2.   Malcolm S. Knowles, A History of the Adult Education Movement in the United States, (Robert E. Krieger, Huntington, NY, 1977).

3.   For this section, I drew extensively on two recent interpretations of the Carnegie Corporation. Amy Deborah Rose, Towards the Organization of Knowledge: Professional Adult Education in the 1920s, doctoral dissertation, Teachers College, Columbia University, 1979; Ellen Condliffe Lagemann, The Politics of Knowledge: The Carnegie Corporation and the Formulation of Public Policy, History of Education Quarterly, 27, 2, (Summer 1987),

pp.205-20.

4.   Lagemann, 'Politics of Knowledge', p.214.

5.   William S. Bernard, 'General Introduction to the Republished Studies', in Frank V. Thompson, Schooling of the Immigrant, (Patterson, Smith, Montclair, NJ, 1971), pp.vii-xlii.

6.   Frank V. Thompson, Schooling of the Immigrant, (Patterson, Smith, Montclair, NJ, 1971).

7.   Ibid, pp.239-41.

8.   William S. Learned, The American Public Library and the Diffusion of Knowledge, (Harcourt, Brace, NY, 1924).

9.   Ibid., p.13.

10.   Frederick P. Keppel, Education for Adults, (Columbia University Press, NY, 1926: Reprinted, Books for Libraries Press, Inc., Freeport, NY, 1968).

11.   Ibid., p.11.

12.   Ibid., p.34.

13.   Ibid., pp.44-50.

14.   Morse A. Cartwright, 'Annual Report of the Director for 1930-31', Journal of Adult Education, (1931), p.1.

15.   Morse A. Cartwright, Annual Report of the Director for 1926-27, (American Association for Adult Education, NY, 1927), p.3.

16.   Morse A. Cartwright, Ten Years of Adult Education: A Report on a Decade of Progress in the American Movement, (Macmillan, NY, 1935), p.39.

17.   Morse A. Cartwright, 'The American Association for Adult Education', Adult Education and the Library, 3, 4, (October 1928), pp.91-103.

18.   Dorothy Canfield Fisher, Why Stop Learning?, (Harcourt, Brace and Company, NY, 1927).

19.   Morse A. Cartwright, Annual Report of the Executive Director, 1927-28, (American Association for Adult Education, NY, 1928), p.20.

20.   Joan Shelley Rubin, 'Self, Culture, and Self-Culture in Modern America: The Early History of the Book-of-the-Month Club', Journal of American History, 71, 4 (March 1985), pp.782-806.

21.   Fisher, Why Stop Learning?, p.4.

22.   Ibid., pp.290-4.

23.   Morse A. Cartwright, 'Annual Report of the Director 1931-32', Journal of Adult Education, 4, (1932), p.1.

24.   For a statement of the radical progressive

approach in adult education, see Ruth Kotinsky, Adult Education and the Social Scene, (D. Appleton-Century Company, Inc., NY, 1933).

25.   Morse A. Cartwright, 'Annual Report of the Director for 1933-34', Journal of Adult Education, 7, (June 1935), pp.2-6.

26.   Morse A. Cartwright, 'Annual Report of the Director for 1934-35', Journal of Adult Education, 17, (June 1983), p.4.

27.   John W. Studebaker, The American Way: Democracy at Work in the Des Moines Forum, (McGraw-Hill, NY, 1935).

28.   Morse A. Cartwright, 'Annual Report of the Director for 1933-34', Journal of Adult Education, 6, (June 1934), p.2.

29.   Cartwright, Ten Years, pp.37-9.

30.   Ibid., p.39.

31.   Alvin S. Johnson, 'After School and College', in Beulah Amidon (ed.), Democracy's Challenge to Education', (Farrar and Rinehart, 1940), pp.132-45.

32.   Dorothy Rowden, 'Morse Adams Cartwright', in J.E. Thomas and Barry Elsey (eds.), International Biography of Adult Education, (Department of Adult Education, University of Nottingham, Nottingham, 1985), pp.82-6.

33.   Edward L. Thorndike, Elsie O. Tilton, J. Warren and Ella Woodyard, Adult Learning, (Macmillan, NY, 1928); Edward L. Thorndike, et. al., Adult Interests, (Macmillan, NY, 1935).

34.   Cartwright, Ten Years, p.33.

35.   Ibid., p.35

36.   For a discussion of Thorndike and the mental testing movement, see Barry M. Franklin, 'Curriculum Thought and Social Meaning: Edward L. Thorndike and the Curriculum Field', Educational Theory, 26, (Summer,1976), pp.298-309.

37.   William S. Gray and Ruth Munroe, Reading Interests and Habits of Adults, (Macmillan, NY, 1929).

38.   Douglas Waples and Ralph W. Tyler, What People Want to Read About, (University of Chicago Press, Chicago, 1931).

39.   Ruth Kotinsky, 'Definition of Felt Needs of Selected Adult Groups in a Community as a Point of Departure in Adult Education', Journal of Educational Sociology, 5, (April 1932) pp.520-2.

40.   Austin H. MacCormick, The Education of Adult

Prisoners: A Survey and a Program, (The National Society of Penal Information, NY, 1931); Benjamin C. Gruenberg, Science and the Public Mind, (McGraw-Hill, NY, 1935); Ira De A. Reid, Adult Education Among Negroes, (The Associates in Negro Folk Education, Washington, DC, 1936); Benson Y. Landis and John D. Willard, Rural Adult Education, (Macmillan, NY, 1933).

41.   R.A. Beals, 'Associated Leadership in Developing a Program of Adult Education', Proceedings of the 20th Annual National University Extension Association, (1935), pp.65-8.

42.   For discussion on the 'service station' approach, see Mary L. Ely (ed.), Adult Education in Action, (American Association for Adult Education, NY, 1936), pp.414-34

43.   'Emergency Education - How Will it Affect the Adult Educational Movement?', Journal of Adult Education, 8, (January 1936), pp.73-8.

44.   Morse A. Cartwright, 'Tolerance in a Democracy', Journal of Adult Education, 11, (June, 1939), pp.235-41.

Chapter Three

LYMAN BRYSON AND THE DEMOCRACY OF CULTURE

Contemporary adult educators know Lyman Bryson (1888-1959) best - if they know him at all - as the author of Adult Education (1), the first textbook of this emerging field of practice. Beginning in the early forties and continuing until his death in 1959, Bryson explored in books as yet not acknowledged as part of the philosophical literature of adult education issues that lay at the heart of the adult education movement: What is the nature of adult education when it is based on a secular world view? To what extent is it really possible to extend culture to the masses?

Bryson came into adult education in mid-life after service with the American Red Cross and the International Red Cross in Europe and Asia from 1918-28, and as Associate Director of the San Diego Museum of Anthropology and Professor of Anthropology at the San Diego State Teachers College. Bryson's career in adult education began in 1929 with his appointment as Executive-Director of the California Association for Adult Education (CAAE). He then served from 1932-34 as Director of the Des Moines, Iowa, Public Forum. In 1934 Bryson moved to New York City to become Professor of Education at Teachers College, Columbia University where he remained until his retirement in 1953. In addition to his work in the graduate adult education program, he established the Readability Laboratory to develop new versions of books on the social sciences.

Bryson foresaw great educational potential in the mass media, and in 1938 he became advisor on adult education and public affairs to the Columbia Broadcasting System. Noted for his work with several programs, he became best known for founding and moderating 'The People's Platform' and 'Invitation to Learning'. From 1949-52 he moderated the religious and ethical TV program, 'Lamp Unto My Feet'.

Bryson's serious intellectual interests found expression in several books and in the prestigious Conference on Science, Philosophy, and Religion in Their Relation to the Democratic Way of Life, which held its first symposium in 1941. Bryson played a leading role in organizing and conducting these annual symposia; he also presented papers at the meetings and prepared, as co-editor, 13 proceedings of these symposia for publication.

When Bryson died in 1959, a career in adult education that spanned some 30 years ended. He left a final legacy, a book published posthumously in 1960, An Outline of Man's Knowledge of the Modern World. (2)

INTERPRETING AND MAPPING ADULT EDUCATION

Bryson (3) identified the material for adult education as the 40 million Americans who were 35 and older and whose educational level was on the seventh and eighth grade. In 1933 only about 27 per cent of American adults who had children in high school themselves had a high school diploma and only half of all adults had gone through the eighth grade. Most adults waited several years between completion of formal schooling and enrolment in adult education programs; few adults under 35 took much interest in continued learning. These individuals had adult responsibilities, but they had little education and little time to get more. Their intelligence had been more formed by their adult experience than by their experiences in abstract reasoning.

Bryson had little doubt about the importance of adult education: any forward movement in society depended upon the communication of the scientific and cultural advances of the minority to the masses. Knowledge could not be 'an esoteric possession of a few'. (4) Not all persons agreed with Bryson's understanding of the nature of this task. The diversity of opinion - even polarization - within the movement manifested itself in a forum dialogue on the aims of adult education that Bryson had with Everett Dean Martin, Director of the People's Institute of New York. (5)

Martin's position on adult education as a form of liberal education was already well-known, and he simply repeated it

43

in this dialogue. Martin limited adult education to education that produced a certain kind of excellence in adults, an excellence that he believed only the elite had the ability to possess. Education for disseminating knowledge or vocational education lay outside the boundary of liberal education.

Bryson, then Forum Leader of the Des Moines Adult Education Project, distanced himself from Martin's restricted understanding. Even vocational or occupational education had, to Bryson, a qualitative dimension when people who studied occupational subjects were interested in becoming better persons through the educational experience. The values of liberal education could be applied to concrete problems which adults confronted in their daily lives. They did not want a pattern of behavior imposed on them; they wanted a character that equipped them to meet whatever circumstances they might confront in their daily lives. Bryson believed the ethical excellence which Martin advocated could be achieved by the masses and not just by an elite few.

Mortimer Adler introduced a version of the Great Books reading plan to the American public in 1940 in How To Read a Book. Bryson praised highly Adler's book and had only slight disagreement about which books to read. (6) But he disagreed with Adler's ideas about beginner books. Only about one million adults in the United States could profit from reading the books on Adler's list; the other Americans would need other assistance before they could profit. In a telling statement, Bryson says: 'Adler appears to be completely incapable of imagining the intellectual processes of an average man who has no teacher nearby to consult'. Bryson was more concerned about helping adults expand their understanding of the world around them through study of specialized fields of knowledge. This task required books that they could read and understand.

Bryson wrote Adult Education, the first textbook of adult education, to provide a systematic account of adult education and to help practitioners to ask the right questions of their experience so that they could work out their own philosophy and methods. What he produced was an accurate representation of the American Association for Adult Education position on adult education as well as his own independent interpretation.

The concept of lifelong learning was not new, but adult education as an organized social movement in American life was new. Bryson believed that three features characterized this new educational movement. First, adult education was a leisure time activity. Bryson defined adult education as 'all the activities with an educational purpose that are carried on by people engaged in the ordinary business of life'. (7) Second, age by itself was not serviceable as a defining factor. A 30-year-old pursuing a doctorate was part of the school system, while a boy 16 who had graduated from high school and continued on his own to enrich his background or refine his occcupational skills was engaging in adult education. Third, adult education was further generally characterized as voluntary, an activity of 'self-direction'. To be sure, some activities such as programs to combat illiteracy might be compulsory. For the most part, however, men and women sought further learning because of 'self-determined' needs discovered in the actual course of living.

Even though adult education was an activity that adults pursued voluntarily in their leisure time as an adjunct to their principal social roles, there were three compelling reasons why adult education required the attention of thoughtful men and women at every level of American society. One reason rested on Bryson's view of education as a necessary social function of the state and society to assist persons to learn the symbols that characterized their culture. A task of education as a social agency was also to give adults the tools of criticism and instruments of reform to remold society.

A second reason was that the adult public had undergone modification. The general educational level had increased, and the age composition had changed. The birth rate had begun to slacken and the average life length was increasing. Adult education became more important when more people were proportionately of older age. The older population faced problems of social and economic reconstruction. But Bryson did not regard adult education as just a response to the present social crisis: a good society provided increased opportunities for self-improvement.

Bryson only dimly perceived what researchers in the sixties and seventies would discover about the stages of adult development, but he recognized that the problems adults confronted varied according to their age. That was a third reason for the necessity of adult education. The personality was not made once and for all. Youth could not be taught to meet problems that they would face at middle age. Growing personalities, Bryson contended, required continuing learning. Thus learning was concurrent with the whole span of life.

Adult education contained a wide variety of subject matter and was sponsored by many agencies, but it was more than the sum total of its parts. It served vital functions in American life. And if it was concurrent with the life span, its scope included all the domains of life. Bryson's classification scheme included five principal functions: remedial, occupational, relational, liberal, and political. Remedial education provided grown up citizens with the minimal skills in literacy, civic knowledge, and homemaking and child care. Occupational education included improvement for present job, advancement to another job, retraining of workers displaced by machines, and guidance for occupational choice or adjustment. Relational education centered on parent education and understanding of self and others. Liberal education described activities that were valuable in themselves, more liberating than instrumental such as remedial or occupational. Political education focused broadly on equipping adults to live in the commonwealth and specifically on the study of politics and political action.

Adult education had many specialized functions and fields of practice, but it had one essential aim: 'a constant growth in independent thinking power and in the capacity for the management of one's own program is an essential aim, implicit in all other purposes'. (8) These various functions were ways in which adults expressed their fundamental motive for self-improvement. The fundamental motive behind all adult learning efforts sprang from the desire to improve one's personality and gain self-direction.

Given intellectual self-improvement as the aim of adult education, then teachers of adults had specific roles that transcended the teaching of subject matter. First, with adults, teachers began with the student's own purposes, not with objectives that lay outside the student. Teachers, however, used the subject matter to lead students to wider interests and to enhance their capacity for 'self-education'.

Second, the teachers were to 'exemplify and teach a rational skepticism', an approach possible only with adults. The young might be taught to criticize the present culture, but they lacked the experience and social status to engage in any social reconstruction. Adults needed more than merely to learn new knowledge. They needed guidance to understand the varied opinions and propaganda that called for their judgment and allegiance. Teachers best served adults by example, by showing how to examine all elements of an argument without resorting to prejudice or invoking faith. This task comprised the primary obligation of the educator of adults. (9)

But a third role had to be addressed. In some instances the teacher also became a leader who produced action in students. Each teacher had to decide the extent to which he or she worked for action. Bryson did not resolve this issue satisfactorily, but he did place the issue in a context that permits resolution. Adult education as part of a social movement had to have social ends, and two kinds of leaders were necessary to achieve these social ends. One kind assisted people to act based on clear thinking and enlightenment. These leaders helped to crystalize and simplify arguments so action could be taken. But the other kind of leader helped people take action. Action was not antithetical to adult education; people wanted to act, not live in the ivory tower. But before people took action, the adult educator's proper role was to help men and women gain wisdom, to clarify their goals and the consequences of such action.

Bryson could not deny the social ends of adult education, but he believed adult education could best serve social ends as an instrument of intellectual improvement and not in directing social change. The test case for him as well as other adult educators came over the issue of workers' education. He rejected workers' education as a unique form of adult education with unique purposes; there should be no special program for workers that differed from the education needed by all adults.

THE NEW PROMETHEAN ENTERPRISE

By the forties Bryson had expanded his interest beyond the nature and organization of adult education to explore the task of adult education in an American society that had become secular - driven by science and technology - and in which large organizations so dominated American life that individuals had little freedom left. In the 1941 Kappa Delta Pi Lecture Series, Bryson claimed that 'every generation of leaders has its own Promethean task', and the task of the present generation was to help men learn from science and not passion. (10)

By 1947 Bryson had developed fully his ideas about the relation of science, culture, and education into a philosophy of scientific humanism. (11) By scientific humanism, Bryson meant 'a philosophy by whose principles we scientifically study and master human behavior for the fulfillment of human powers'. (12) And he wanted judgments to be made about human behavior that were secular, made without justification or appeal to religious systems. Scientific inquiry was a moral activity guided by moral rules in which judgments were made in the public world where men could seek agreement. Secular judgments did not mean the absence of values. Scientific knowledge was directed toward ends derived from a value system: democracy. In democracy, the highest value is freedom, a human good that allowed creative energies to find fullest expression. Democracy required a society with plural values so that a variety of loyalties could be nourished and change made quickly but with rational controls.

Using scientific knowledge to better human life was a complex process involving several steps. A critical step entailed distinguishing between the research and engineering aspects of science; their functions differed. Social scientists created dependable knowledge for its own sake, but its application required social engineering. In mature science, the problems of theory and the problems of use were distinguished. The researcher used a method and accepted the results; the engineer used all methods to get a predetermined result. (13)

Bryson's distinction between research and engineering differed, he acknowledged, from that of Robert Lynd's, a well-known sociologist who had wrestled with the same problem in an earlier and well-known book, Knowledge for What? The Place of Social Science in American Culture. (14) Bryson agreed with Lynd's diagnosis that social scientists had mistakenly separated knowledge from value, but he disagreed with Lynd's conclusion that the remedy would emerge from studying society and creating knowledge about it.

To the contrary, many areas of scientific advance required the co-operation of lay people. In public health, for example, research in the laboratory came first, followed by an engineering phase to change the environment, and then co-operation in which lay people learned the rules. Without acknowledging that he is doing so, Bryson returns to the original Carnegie Corporation idea of the diffusion of knowledge. In Bryson's argument, adult education was the final phase of the research and development process. Bryson was concerned about what came later to be called the applied behavioral sciences.

Science aided social engineering by describing human behavior in such precise terms that statistical predictions could be made. In Bryson's argument, greatly simplified, when two persons formed complementary relationships, they created an institution, and a pattern of institutions created a culture. From these relations, persons derived their self-respect and opportunities for self-expression. They, in short, acquired loyalties to these relationships and to the institutions in which these relationships were formed and sustained. In the course of their life, different persons acquired different loyalties. Only a democracy - but not other political systems - would permit these plural loyalties to develop. At the point of these loyalties - the emotions of individuals - the social engineer intervened.

Adults lived in a constantly changing network of influences (a flow of symbols) that constantly modified or changed their behavior pattern. Agents of change - whether a social engineer motivated by scientific humanism or a charismatic demagogue such as Hitler - worked with these influences - symbols - and they modified and changed these influences through education and persuasion. Education built up the original habit pattern; persuasion influenced the older pattern. The social engineer used education to build habits of free action, loyalties to the institutions of freedom.

Bryson's search for the relation of science to the realization of human values coalesced in his vision of the Good Society. (15) The Good Society permitted the largest numbers of its members to attain the ends which that society valued. Bryson wanted to avoid utopian absolutes that prescribed unattainable aims. Instead, a successful society presented aims to individuals attainable by human nature, provided institutional patterns that inculcated these values, and made opportunities available for their attainment. (16) A good society permitted men to change their institutional loyalties without the cost of suffering. A good society was a tolerant society.

Bryson made the success of each society a matter of investigation and judgment, a problem to be studied as any other social problem. One began such a study by objectively describing the society's standard of success, the means provided to attain that standard, and how this complete pattern would likely survive in relation to other cultural influences to which it had to be subjected. Thus informed, the social engineer then diagnosed how well a particular society had attained its goals and prescribed more efficient means to close the gap between achievements and ideals.

Bryson had hoped that his vision of the Good Society could, in fact, become reality. Toward the end of his career, he expressed in the Fund for Adult Education Lecture Series, his belief that the areas in human life in which reason was used instead of tradition were enlarging. (17) More questions in American culture were being answered by the facts and values involved and less by what people thought custom dictated.

The question remained, however, whether the American people could accept the conclusions of the social sciences and act on those conclusions. They were prevented from accepting social science knowledge and the method of scientific thinking by attitudes - theirs and the social scientists - toward science as a human activity. Scientists and engineers described and manipulated the material universe, but they had not concerned themselves with values. With regard to values, Bryson believed that higher education fared no better. Professors gave students a knowledge of the secular world.

Bryson himself embraced a secular world view. But secularism, he recognized, presented a profound challenge to thoughtful people: what kind of standards can be determined by reason freed from tradition and fear? In a secular society rational, not supernatural, explanations were sought to explain the events of human experience in the present. Bryson wanted to extend rational explanations to explain the events in human history that had been previously explained as divine revelations. Bryson believed that a philosophy or moral system could be founded on rational grounds. Scientific ways of thinking did not destroy moral values. To the contrary, persons derived values from reflection on experience. In this enterprise, scientific thinking provided a tool as useful for ethical and moral work as for other areas of human action.

Science had given a way by which men and women could be free without being conformed to one pattern of life. At mid-twentieth century, all men and women - not just an elite few - were expected to use their reason. That was the great achievement. But an equally great educational task remained to be resolved: to develop a way of life in which all citizens learned all their lives and used their minds.

THE DEMOCRATIZATION OF CULTURE

The United States had undergone a transition to the Great Economy in which collectives ruled and individuals were left powerless to control their lives. Bryson despaired of this new direction of American life. He wrote The Next America as his diagnosis and prescription to make this transition as harmless as possible and to find other avenues to preserve or restore values lost in the process. (18)

Return to an earlier, less complex period was not possible. That organized groups ruled by the majority was a necessary part of democratic life was not disputed. But institutions - almost as a law of their nature - increasingly included more functions under their purview and took over more aspects of the lives of their employees or members. Employers provided recreation, family counseling, and sometimes political advice for their employees. Churches, too, had extended their interests into areas of human life other than religion. In American life, three collectives - corporations, labor unions, and government - dominated. In none of these did the individual have any power or creative outlets. New areas of democratic action and freedom had to be found.

The Next America that Bryson envisioned was really the Next Democracy. Democracy had as its end not the state, not the political party, not an ideal, but the human being. More than a political process, democracy entailed an educational process: a theory of learning by choice.

A democratic system required freedom in the area of knowledge: free people had to be trained, informed, and educated. They needed to be trained in co-operative action to have respect for differences in persons, tolerance, social sportsmanship, and social skill. They needed to be informed about the world so that ignorance did not blind their imagination. They needed to be educated to know what could be learned from the experiences of others.

In the United States at the mid-twentieth century, democracy could not be found in the corporation, labor unions, or government. Bryson located the experience of the democratic life elsewhere: the individual, the personal management of community, and 'the democracy of culture'.

The reality of democratic life, Bryson maintained, had

always been the individual's inner development and spiritual strength. In the individual lay the means of personal freedom and the activities to help individuals realize their freedom. In the democracy of culture 'no vehicle of living, no institution or skill can be an end in itself'. (19) The highest end was experience. Persons should seek the highest quality of experience, and in politics, arts, and the sciences persons found the instruments of humanity to obtain a better life. The new democracy would not be built on external institutions but in the 'inwardly organized soul of human beings'. (20)

Bryson had no patience with the argument that the self could be realized only in dedication to some cause that required commitment and sacrifice. German youths were committed to Hitler, but they were also misguided and caused harm to the world. The standard had to be the effects on the individual and not whether the institution prospered. Problems occurred when people believed that they had to make a permanent commitment to these institutions. When people assigned them 'external reality', objectified them, they came to believe they existed for the state, the church, the profession, or the club. In Bryson's doctrine of individualism, the end of living was the development of one's higher powers, and the chief means of that was learning from free choice and consequences.

Freedom could also be realized in the personal management of communities: the core of political democracy. Participation in a geographical community provided opportunity to exercise individual judgments, to take action with others, and to learn by 'the lesson of events'. But more important than taking action, such participation in community life provided opportunity for discussion. To Bryson, discussion provided practice in the methods implemented in the democratic political process. Discussion became a testing place for democracy by sharpening people's powers of thinking and engaging them in decision-making. Even if no action resulted discussion had benefits. In discussion the majority had to listen to the minority; this discipline inculcated in the majority a sportsman-like friendliness toward minorities, whether minorities of race, ethnic origin, or religion. Such sportsmanship was necessary for actual living in the community.

The most novel and radical of Bryson's ideas for creative outlets reached beyond individualism and personal

management of community to 'the democracy of culture'.
(21) In a democracy of culture, all men and women would
engage in creating the culture within the powers of their
ability as well as enjoying it. In taking this position, Bryson
challenged the elite theory of culture. In the elite theory of
culture, a gifted few created the great things of the human
spirit, and their creations were collected by a few who then
made them available to the rest of the population. (22)
Bryson based his idea of 'the democracy of culture' upon
other assumptions. He wanted to admit everyone to the
enjoyment of culture because only through personal
experience could they find out for themselves the things
worth knowing and enjoying. The cultural heritage could not
be learned without contact; people had to learn their
culture.

There were problems, however, in realizing this ideal.
Authorities on civilization and cycles of taste contended
that in society there were periods of achievement and
periods of enjoyment, and these periods did not occur at the
same time. Nevertheless, Bryson wanted to shorten the lag
between achievement and enjoyment. What he proposed was
an experiment that had no past experience to provide
guidance. He wanted, in effect, to use art and thought to
further democratic experience in which the citizens thought
of themselves as creators.

Mass culture - the popular term for the 'democracy of
culture' - offended many critics who could only think of
mass culture as vulgar taste. But Bryson challenged the
critics: mass culture did not necessarily result in vulgar
taste. With the advent of the machine age, art objects such
as paintings, plays, and books were produced for the masses
and widely disseminated. Much of the public's taste was
vulgar, Bryson conceded, but it was vulgar because the
public had more opportunities for personal choice. In the
long run, however, the process would serve to elevate taste.

The elevation of taste would not occur immediately, for
there were stages of cultural freedom when people had
choice. A first stage would be 'vulgarity' in which people
explored without any standards to guide them. In the second,
the people would develop taste, appreciation, and standards.
In the third stage - a stage necessary for a democracy of
culture to be achieved - the people would create their own
art. The results might be less than fully satisfying to the
purists, but the democracy of culture, like the democracy of
politics, sought to include every person in the experience

rather than guard the practical results. People must have freedom to make mistakes and to choose wrongly.

In the democracy of culture, experience, not some abstract ideal, was the real measure. Some critics assessed the value of contemporary products against the standards of some absolute values or they rated historical cultures by the art and literary objects or the institutions it left behind. But to Bryson the real test of any culture remained the daily experience of the people, what the culture gave them in their daily lives.

THE NEW TASKS OF EDUCATION

Education was the most elaborate set of institutions that a culture used to mold and remold the minds of people. (23) In this conception, education could not be equated with the experience of life itself; it was, rather 'our organized ways of learning from the experience of others', Bryson described education as 'institutional behavior that provides opportunities for purposeful learning'.

In society education had three purposes. Education, first, transmitted culture - accumulated knowledge - from one generation to another. Education, secondly, worked for the critical revision of culture but not by attempting to build a new social order as the radical progressives had advocated in the thirties. Schools could do only what culture allowed, but organized education was not without influence. It influenced the future by the ideas and loyalties it inculcated in its members. Bryson regarded social change as the group aspect of individual change. But a third purpose had resulted from the experience of the second world war. Attention had been focused on the international community and the role of education in preparing persons for life in the international context. Bryson called this purpose 'enlightenment' in which persons moved beyond 'nationalism', beyond the concept of 'enemy' to 'human being'.

How persons should be trained to live in American culture was the subject of unending argument. (24) Part of the difficulty stemmed from different ideas about the function of the state. Bryson took for his own position the classical idea of the state that came from the Greeks through Roman law and medieval theory. The classical idea - best expressed in Plato's Republic - regarded 'the state as a normative agency, shaping its citizens to a preordained ideal'. In the United States this idea found expression in Thomas Jefferson's separation of church and state and Horace Mann's ideas of the common school that made the state the primary agent in education.

A second idea of the state - also strong in American thought and practice - came from the Teutonic tradition that began not with the state but with our self which can be imagined in freedom. The classic statement was John Stuart Mill, Essay on Liberty. Mill denied the state the right to educate the child against the wishes of parents; laws and governments were not instruments to create free individuals.

Indeed, Bryson agreed, society existed for its members who were not to be manipulated by its rulers. But Bryson believed, as Mill did not, that the state and its legislative apparatus could be the means to make men free: government performed this function through public education. Other influences on the young - the family, the peer group, and the ideas of heroism communicated by the media - competed with the schools, but the school remained the decisive influence in training persons to be free.

Making self-government a norm also entailed helping youth make the transition from the family as a single group to the multiple groups that adults had to contend with. Society started children in life by teaching them that there was one good way of doing things. They were then turned out into a pluralistic, industrial society where they had to make decisions. The schools and peer group mediated a fixed pattern of behavior which youth were expected to remain loyal to in adult life.

There were other and better ways of making citizens, however. Bryson agreed that persons needed loyalty to special patterns by which they lived, but they also needed habits and skills of freedom and loyalty to the idea of freedom itself. To bring this about in children and youth required that the teacher exercise self-restraint and skill in explanation. From their superior knowledge, teachers - as the 'deputy of culture' - arranged experiences for the students to develop the qualities society wanted. Children and youth learned to be free by practice only when the teacher was a guide, not a master. Children and youth grew toward freedom with graded-levels of experience.

Unlike children and youth, adults no longer saw going to school as their job. They did, however, go on learning, either accidentally and without plan, or systematically and deliberately when the resources of the community were offered. Adults, too, were guided into experiences through which they became aware of what they wanted to know. They were helped by teachers who assisted them to see their problems in a broad context and to identify the knowledge that was relevant to them.

In The Drive Toward Reason, Bryson argued that Americans were driven by the passion to better themselves and by the belief that society must be judged by the lives of average men and women and not by the special achievements of the elite. These passions were the 'natural strength of what we call adult education'. Adult education as a means for bettering ourselves had become so 'pervasive and fundamental a part of our way of life' that it was beyond the range of public schools and professional educators and it no longer needed a name.

This widespread acceptance of education as a lifelong process had not alleviated critical problems in diffusing knowledge to the masses, to the adult population. (25) For one, too few institutions devoted their efforts to the growth of personalities. Many groups promoting so-called 'public purposes' had preconceived conditions and directions for growth; these groups served regressive ends and provided no opportunity for adults to grapple with real issues. Lectures, study groups, and readings engaged adults at one level of intensity, but these methods failed to engage adults in 'the sweaty struggle of real learning'. Only adults intently involved in personal and social affairs engaged in learning that brought about change.

Even more important than this problem was one that Bryson addressed often: the failure to develop experts in the diffusion of knowledge to adults. Bryson, like James Harvey Robinson, called for a new educational role. In the western world, there had emerged three types of educators. Primary and secondary school teachers passed on what they found in books. Scholars conducted research and trained apprentices but they did not routinely translate their research for the general public. Managers of educational and social service institutions provided services, but they did not take responsibility for the dissemination of knowledge. Each of these types played important roles in education, but none interpreted knowledge for the general public.

The general public did not lack interpreters. But these interpreters - usually experts in their field - lacked training or experience in pedagogy. Thus the public depended on newspaper and magazine writers to interpret the physical sciences, reporters to interpret political affairs, and lecturers and priests to interpret moral and social issues. Scientists generally did not aid these interpreters in their work; scientists only got involved when they recognized the need for the support of an enlightened public. Scientists did not consider interpretation a career.

For the public, then, the function of interpretation was served by accident and without any special selection or training of the interpreters. While Bryson decried the absence of interpreters, he could not describe the skills interpreters would need or what elements would be contained in the 'psychology of free learning'.

Even if a new educational career of interpreter of scientific knowledge for the general public did emerge, there still remained the problem of leadership and agencies of mediation between the scientific community and the general public. Bryson searched for historical and contemporary solutions. What he sought was a way to permit persons of knowledge to pursue careers combined with a larger social function. A healthy society made it possible for men's purposes - making a living and gaining a reputation - to converge with their social functions - serving some social good. Bryson wanted to modify the system so that careers in community leadership would be satisfying and attractive, but such careers required an agency of mediation - 'the tool of leadership and the vehicle of careers'. (26)

At one time the church had been the agency to mediate culture and at other times statesmen and political leaders had performed this function. Leadership could be found in government, but Bryson did not regard the government as a likely agency. However, two projects in the depression - the Works Progress Administration and the Tennessee Valley Authority - pointed out possible directions. Nor did Bryson expect leadership to come from labor unions; union leaders spoke for and served their unions' purposes, not national purposes.

Bryson saw emerging 'a new and experimental institution' - a new national agency of mediation - that could serve the function of cultural mediation: the public high school. (27) Why the public high school? It was the one institution in American society by which future citizens would be shaped; by 1947 54 per cent of the population had graduated from high school. Every citizen had access to it on the same terms, and the public controlled it. Bryson projected a new role for this community agency, but he provided neither a rationale nor programmatic suggestions for such an undertaking.

NOTES

1. Lyman Bryson, Adult Education, (American Book Company, NY, 1936).
2. Lyman Bryson, (ed.), An Outline of Man's Knowledge of the Modern World, (Nelson Doubleday, Garden City, NY, 1960).
3. Lyman Bryson, 'For Whom are we Working?', Journal of Adult Education, 5, (April 1933), pp.136-40.
4. Ibid., p.138.
5. Lyman Bryson and Everett Dean Martin, 'To Educate Everybody: A Forum Dialogue on the Aims of Adult Education', Journal of Adult Education, 6, (October 1934), pp.395-9.
6. Lyman Bryson, 'Oh-Go Read a Book!', Journal of Adult Education, 12, (June 1940), pp.284-9.
7. Bryson, Adult Education, pp.3-4.
8. Ibid., p.31.
9. Ibid., pp.63-5.
10. Lyman Bryson, The New Prometheus, (Macmillan, NY, 1941), p.1.
11. Lyman Bryson, Science and Freedom, (Columbia University Press, NY, 1947).
12. Ibid., p.xi.
13. Ibid., pp.77-9.
14. Robert S. Lynd, Knowledge for What? The Place of Social Science in American Culture, (Princeton University Press, Princeton, 1939).
15. Lyman Bryson, 'What is a Good Society?', in Lyman Bryson and Louis Finkelstein (eds.), Science, Philosophy, and Religion, (Third Symposium of the Conference on Science, Philosophy, and Religion, 1943; Kraus Reprint Company, NY, 1971), pp.145-62.
16. Bryson, Science and Freedom, p.173.
17. Lyman Bryson, The Drive Toward Reason: In the Service of a Free People, (Harper, NY, 1954).
18. Lyman Bryson, The Next America: Prophecy and Faith, (Harper, NY, 1952).
19. Ibid., p.112.
20. Ibid.

21. Ibid., p.101.

22. For an analysis of these issues similar to Bryson's see also Herbert J. Gans, Popular Culture and High Culture: An Analysis and Evaluation of Taste, (Basic Books, NY, 1974).

23. Bryson, Science and Freedom, pp.117-18.

24. Bryson, The Drive Toward Reason, pp.19-39.

25. Bryson, Science and Freedom, pp.133-43.

26. Bryson, The Next America, pp.180-6.

27. Ibid., p.183.

Part II

ADULT EDUCATION AS LIBERAL EDUCATION

Chapter Four

EVERETT DEAN MARTIN AND A GROWN-UP CIVILIZATION

Many of these who attempted to create an identity for adult education as a unique form or level of education derived the unifying principle from the liberal education tradition. They attempted to create adult education in the image of liberal education. In the twenties, when the adult education movement began, Everett Dean Martin (1880-1941) was the first to publish a major book within this tradition. In 1924 Martin was among those Frederick Keppel invited to the preliminary conference to explore a possible role for the Carnegie Corporation in adult education, and he participated actively in the activities of the American Association for Adult Education.

Martin held a narrow definition of liberal education. Many in the adult education movement disagreed with his belief in the centrality of liberal education. At the 1936 celebration of ten years of the American Association for Adult Education, Martin voiced his fear: 'There is apparently some danger that the liberal concept of education may come to be regarded as merely a cult or faction of the adult education movement in America'. (1)

Martin came into adult education after a brief career in the ministry. From 1906 to 1914 he held pastorates in Congregational and Unitarian churches, but in 1914 he left the ministry to devote full-time to writing about social issues.

In 1916 Martin was appointed a lecturer of social philosophy at the People's Institute in New York City. Giving his first course of lectures on psychology, Martin proved to be a popular lecturer. The next year he was appointed Director of the Cooper Union Forum and

Assistant Director of the People's Institute. In 1922 he became Director, a position he held until 1934 when the People's Institute closed for lack of funds. The Cooper Union took over the adult lecture series and established the Department of Social Philosophy with Martin as Head. In 1938 Martin took a faculty appointment as professor of social philosophy at the Claremont Graduate School in Claremont, California.

Martin's almost a quarter of a century career in adult education was focused around his commitment to liberal education - the humanist tradition - as the unifying philosophy of adult education. Martin expounded his philosophy in twelve books on social psychology, social philosophy, politics, and adult education, testing the ideas first as lectures. He proved adept at interpreting to a lay public complex social science concepts and social issues in the light of historical examples and the humanist tradition. His books were non-fiction best sellers. In recognition of his wide interests, his biographers have called him an adult educator, a sociologist, a social psychologist, and social theorist.

THE PEOPLE'S INSTITUTE: THE SETTING OF A CAREER

The People's Institute where Martin's career in adult education unfolded had been founded by Charles Spraque Smith in 1897 and the first lectures offered on March 17, 1898 at the Cooper Union. While Professor of Modern Languages and Foreign Literature at Columbia College (now Columbia University), Smith became dissatisfied with the cultivated and genteel life at Columbia and its isolation from New York City life. His attempts to get Columbia College involved in elevating the cultural life of the city failed, and in 1891 he resigned from Columbia to devote his life to social reform. (2)

Smith wanted to educate the immigrants and native Americans in a cultural tradition foreign to both: the cultural tradition of the American 'aristocracy'. Smith intended to make this cultural tradition 'the high culture for the masses, the culture of democratic humanism'. (3) This humanist tradition had its origin in Athenian Greece, had been rediscovered and elaborated in the Renaissance, and further developed in the Enlightenment. Martin later expounded this tradition in his lectures, books, and articles.

The People's Institute of New York City was part of a larger reform movement in the nation to elevate the working class and the immigrants. The movement began with the settlement house, and other People's Institutes had been organized in Boston and Chicago prior to the one in New York City. Other New York City organizations with similar intentions included The Free Lecture System directed by Henry M. Leipziger, the Educational Alliance, and the Cooper Union.

Smith promoted his 'democratic humanism' through several programs. The People's Church, a Sunday evening program on ethics and religion, attempted to overcome differences based on religion. Smith also organized clubs of working men and sought to make culture uplifting as well as entertaining through art, concerts, and dance performances. After the defeat of the reform candidate for mayor in 1897, Smith organized the People's Forum to counter corrupt government and to develop virtuous citizens. Calling his program 'progressive democracy', Smith wanted to return government to the republican ideal; he wanted government by intelligent and responsible leaders who were controlled by and responsive to the needs and desires of an educated citizenry. To achieve this, Smith held mass meetings on issues, took straw votes, had public officials report on their conduct, and printed a journal.

The first phase of the People's Institute ended with Smith's death in 1910. Beginning in 1910 the People's Institute entered the community organization phase and began the use of scientific methods - surveys, investigations, social science experiments, and urban planning - for social improvement. As part of this effort, the People's Institute established the New York Training School for Community Workers and conducted a major study on the causes of juvenile delinquency. The People's Institute also entered the leisure-time field with the organization of social centers in the New York City public schools.

Under Martin's leadership the People's Institute concentrated on adult education. It shifted from involvement in the movement for scientific efficiency and urban and environmental improvement to focus on the creation of an adult population that was rational and humanist. Martin's personal orientation was obviously one reason for this shift, but the shift from emphasis on the social to the individual reflected a change in American society as a whole. This change had also effected another

New York City institution, the New School for Social Research. After the war the United States retreated from the reform interest, both at home and abroad. The interests of audiences changed from social, economic, and political interests to a hunger for knowledge itself and for historical and philosophical analysis of these events. Another factor was finances. A community organization program could not be maintained by subscriptions alone, and after the war external funds were not available.

Martin implemented his adult education ideas through lecture series, the School of Philosophy, and the Reader Roundtable Discussion Groups. Martin limited the work of the People's Institute at the Cooper Union to lectures and discussions on Tuesday, Friday and Sunday evenings. The musical and dance programs were discontinued, and its post-war forums did not attempt to influence current legislation, did not hold mass meetings on specific issues, and did not take straw votes. For the Tuesday and Sunday evening lectures, Martin enlisted the leading intellectuals in New York City as lecturers.

A popular lecturer himself, Martin conducted the Friday evening lecture series. He had the ability to appeal to the lay mind. He used direct and forceable language, and he broke down difficult subject matter into digestible and interesting forms for persons who had little formal education. He used these Friday night lectures to work out his ideas and to expound his social and philosophical position.

Many in the audience wanted to have more contact with Martin and to study the liberal art subjects in a smaller classroom setting. In the fall of 1917, the School of Philosophy was organized at the request of students at Martin's Friday night lectures. Designed to offer students a humanist education, the program featured lectures that were primarily philosophical, treating the history of ideas and their relevance to the present. The instructors had to have a humanist viewpoint, and the People's Institute used the most able college professors in New York City. The School met the first year on Saturday evenings at the Cooper Union but moved to community locations the next year. The program was increased to four evenings each week and prominent lecturers such as Mortimer Adler and Scott Buchanan became part of the faculty. Working unofficially with the American Library Association, the School moved in 1928 to the Muhlenberg Branch of the New York Public

Library.

In 1926, in co-operation with the American Association for Adult Education and the Carnegie Corporation, the People's Institute organized small study groups of ten to 16 members located at various sites in the city. The Reader Roundtable Discussion Groups' program was an experimental study of small reading groups to test alternatives to lectures, to test methods of group discussion, and to identify the best group discussion methods for adult education.

The Readers Roundtable offered two types of courses. One type was designed for adults with interest in specific subjects such as the Fine Arts, Drama, or Labor. The second was modeled after the General Honors Course at Columbia University initiated by Professor John Erskine in 1921. This course acquainted members through readings and Socratic discussions with the works of authors who had shaped western civilization. Both types of courses addressed the same purposes; they were cultural, not vocational, and for the intellectually serious students who would agree to read each day. The classes had two leaders, one with a literary and one with a philosophical background. Most of the instructors came from Columbia University, including Whitaker Chambers, Moses Hadas, Richard McKeon, Phillip Yountz, Clifton Fadiman, Scott Buchanan, and Mortimer Adler.

In 1929 Martin proposed that the activities of the People's Institute become part of the Cooper Union. The Cooper Union agreed to the proposal but with the stipulation that the transfer be made when it could afford it. In 1934, the Carnegie Corporation offered $15,000 per year for three years to support the transition. The Cooper Union agreed and established the Department of Social Philosophy with Martin as the Director. (4)

MARTIN'S SOCIAL AND POLITICAL PHILOSOPHY: OR WHAT IS WRONG WITH AMERICA

Martin's prescription of liberal education - the humanistic tradition - addressed specific problems that he believed were prevalent in American society. His first book, The Behavior of Crowds, was published in 1920 after a time of mass hysteria in the United States about foreign influences. (5) In this book Martin staked out an agenda and a perspective that occupied him for the rest of his career.

Martin chose to work on the psychological frontier, for to him the psychological forces that threatened society were more important than economic ones. He identified crowd behavior as the critical psychological problem. The problem was not conflict between the individual and society; they were not irreconcilable nor were they abstractions to be pitted against one another. Instead, the conflict grew out of the relationships between individuals and groups.

Drawing upon Le Bon's The Crowd and Freud's theory of psychoanalysis, particularly in The Interpretation of Dreams and Totem and Taboo, Martin described group behavior as a 'class of psychological phenomena' characterized by unconscious motivation, the same phenomena as dreams, delusions, and other forms of automatic behavior. A crowd developed a belief - its particular illusion, ideal, or dream - and excluded all other contradictory ideas and opinions. One kind of crowd, perhaps the best known, was the street crowd or mob whose behavior often resulted in violent acts such as lynchings. But other kinds of crowds disturbed Martin even more. One of these was mass meetings. Martin saw manifestations of this on occasions at the Cooper Union when members of the audience began to cite slogans without thinking through the meaning of the ideas. This kind of behavior was particularly likely to occur at political rallies. Most alarming to Martin were special interest groups or organizations, what he called the 'struggle groups', formed to perpetuate some belief or principle. Martin did not regard as wrong the efforts of groups or factions to get their ideas accepted and to become the controlling force in society. But such behavior often became pathological: the believer sought to vindicate rather than verify the ideas and to preserve his belief at any cost. Civilizing influences had not penetrated very deeply into human nature. The primitive urges in persons never die: in the crowd the 'primitive ego' got its wishes and gained control of part of society.

From the perspective of crowd behavior, Martin criticized several aspects of American life. So strongly did he denounce crowd behavior in American democracy that commentators have called him anti-democratic. (6) As Martin read the political scene, democracy appeared to be threatened by the excess of crowd behavior. Factions sought to use the government to extend their powers and influence, exercising what de Tocqueville called 'the tyranny of the majority', a phrase that Martin quoted with approval. When the crowd sought to extend its powers over private practices, the Constitution was necessary to limit the tyranny of the crowd.

A society characterized by crowd behavior threatened the existence of civilization, for it made 'the achievement of personality and true knowledge of self' impossible. People could not come to know themselves when they were compelled to take sides. When crowd behavior prevailed, every interest degenerated into propaganda, advertising techniques, sloganeering, and attempts to persuade others to follow. The newspaper, the leader in crowd-thinking, perpetuated the crowd mind by appealing to the lowest level of thinking.

In the twenties, Martin used crowd behavior as a perspective from which to interpret behavior in American society. In the thirties he addressed a problem that may have been autobiographical but it occupied others as well: the problem of belief in the modern world. In Civilizing Ourselves Martin examined the historical facts by which the world had become modern and how intellectual maturity could be achieved. (7) Martin dated the beginning of the modern world with the Renaissance which ushered in a secular civilization free of ecclesiastical authority. In this interpretation Martin did not engage in original scholarship but reworked standard materials. The importance of his interpretation lay not in the originality of his scholarship but in the central problem that he identified for adult education.

For 400 years the world had been undergoing a cultural revolution, described by Martin as the 'greatest spiritual and cultural revolution of all times'. (8) But no new cultural center emerged to replace the culture of the medieval Catholic Church. The Renaissance began a task the modern world needed to complete: to be truly skeptical of the continued manifestation of religion and to develop a hierarchy of values appropriate for a secular culture. The task was to 'modernize' the 'thinking' of adults. Adult intelligence in the modern world required becoming conscious of what it was to believe anything. (9)

Martin wanted to find a conception of spirituality appropriate for a secular culture. By culture he meant 'a vast socially accepted system of preferences'. Martin called the problem of western civilization 'a spiritual problem' but not a religious problem in the traditional sense.

Persons could attain the spiritual life in several ways. Those who chose to renounce the world acted on the belief in dualism: they denied matter in the interest of spirit. Others chose Naturalism or Romanticism in the belief that spirit and nature were one. To them pursuing the spiritual life meant to throw off the abnormalities of civilization and be themselves. Martin regarded Rousseau as the best example of this philosophy, and Martin denounced Rousseau in this book and in other writings as the arch villain of western civilization. Martin objected to Romanticism's championing the cause of the masses, its idealization of the common man. Romanticism made a hierarchy of values impossible, for distinctions of worth necessary for civilization could not be derived from Nature.

Rejecting both dualism and Romanticism, Martin called his approach mental maturity. This better way transformed both the 'raw material of experience and the earlier infantile ideas of spirituality as one grows up'. (10) By spirituality Martin meant what man had done to give meaning to nature and living. It recognized persons as choosing beings, as capable of facing facts - dealing with reality - and making critical distinctions. In transforming social and economic realities into an order of preferences and values, some used the method of adolescence by finding security in fancy and fiction. Children, philosophers, religious people, neurotics, and a nation of half-mature people found security this way, but not adults.

A secular culture did not allow retreat to religious dogma for the source of meaning. All that persons had been given was the world of fact which they transformed into meaning through symbols and fictions. Martin permitted no explanations based on belief in divine origins. The world of institutions, religions, philosophy, and science were human creations which transformed the economic and biological through fictions. Martin used several terms to describe adults who lived by the postulates of secular civilization: 'self-directing mature human beings', 'the grown-up man', 'truly civilized adult living', 'the adult mind', and 'the civilized adult'. (11)

The emergence of a secular civilization was, to Martin, the primary historical fact in the formation of the modern world. But a second historical fact in this formation also concerned Martin: the emergence of the common man, which as a 'type of human being' appeared in the eighteenth century. Martin's attitude toward common people was paradoxical. On the one hand, he worked with them for almost a quarter of a century, and he held out adult education as their hope. But on the other hand, he held them in contempt, did not believe them capable of governing themselves, and wanted them governed by an intellectual leadership of the cultured.

The intellectual leadership of the cultured began its decline in the American and French revolutions - triumphs of the common man - that established the natural rights of man. Andrew Jackson's election as President in 1828 completed the revolution. Until then, the poulation had been under the leadership of 'its most distinguished and cultivated members'. (12) For Martin, Jackson's election marked a watershed in American life in which the character of the nation changed and changed for the worst. Leadership in religion and business as well as politics had been transferred from the educated to the masses. (13)

The idea of America as the nation with the new start supported aspirations of the common man to make the world in his own image. He had done so, but at a terrible cultural cost. In Martin's thesis, the cultural tradition of the United States had been made by one class of people. His bias was obvious: 'Here for the first time in all history a type of man became articulate, pre-eminent, who everywhere else in historic times were subordinate to a traditional ruling class, a hierarchy or an aristocracy.' (14)

When the masses ruled in a democracy, negative consequences followed, and these, he believed, could be seen in the preoccupations of the American people in the last ten years. The government and the 'mob' had led a political heresy hunt to root out the 'reds' and other subversives. The American people had turned against Woodrow Wilson - Martin called him the great political leader - and rejected the League of Nations. The Ku Klux Klan had revitalized the new nation idea. The movement for prohibition sought to impose the control of the masses. Journalism had become the 'instructor of the newly literate masses'. (15)

Philosophers from Plato had feared the rabble, which they equated with the common people. But Martin had a deeper fear: the crowd mentality permeated all of society. 'It is organized and standardized and comes to us with our newspaper at the breakfast table, it speaks from the pulpit and the lecture platform, and is entrenched in the schoolhouse.' (16) As he saw it in 1932, neither businessmen, politicians, nor men in the street were capable of providing leadership. The present experiment in democracy might have to end and the 'intelligent minority' assume leadership. (17)

Another tenent Martin held was belief in individual liberty. (18) Liberty had to do with concrete issues and how to gain specific rights; liberty was hard to define but could be known by what was opposite it. In the Renaissance liberty took the form of freedom to study classic literature, in the Protestant Reformation the right of private interpretation of Scripture, and in the English Revolution the restriction on the power of the monarchy over subjects. This view of liberty was realistic and based on experience, stood for self-discipline and individual responsibility, regarded individual and civil liberties as a human achievement, and viewed liberty as an outcome of, and means to, culture.

This older, classical view of liberty had been replaced by a second philosophy of liberty. Coming into western thought by way of Rousseau, this new conception viewed liberty in general - as a state of human happiness - and not with concrete issues. This philosophy regarded liberty as idealistic and based on emotion, as a natural right, an escape from the artificialities and restraints of civilization. With respect to government, this view of liberty called for the people to rule. When people owned the government, freedom would come by natural good. (19)

TOWARD A THEORY OF LIBERAL EDUCATION FOR ADULTS

Martin first presented his theory of humanistic education for adults in 1920 as the conclusion of his book on The Behavior of Crowds. Crowd behavior threatened the very foundations of civilization, and he wanted some cure for it. He disavowed any single path to social redemption, but he believed that the social condition could be improved. Democracy could be freed from crowd behavior 'by liberating our own thinking'. (20) Such liberation took 'self-analysis and intellectual courage', and Martin identified several persons who in history had exemplified this behavior: Socrates, Protagoras, Peter Abelard, Erasmus, Montaigne, Cervantes, Samuel Butler, Goethe, Emerson, and William James. As psychoanalysis was therapy for neurosis so the process of liberating individual thinking was therapy for crowd behavior. No social change could occur as long as people took refuge in systems of ideas.

Martin prescribed humanistic education as the therapy.

Humanistic education included both the sciences and the humanities, but study of the sciences and humanities only became humanistic as they liberated human intelligence and sympathy. Science as humanistic study - 'a means of freedom - that is, science as culture' - went beyond theory to practical application, to the ends which science pursued and how it enriched human experience. (21) Knowledge of ancient civilization through the classics, when properly studied, helped students to discriminate, to acquire a sense of values, and to become independent in their thinking. (22)

The humanist method as the antidote to crowd behavior made individuals responsible for dealing with concrete reality. In the 'humanist theories of knowledge', ideas were instruments for adjusting to life, human experience was real, the intellect was an instrument of acting, and truth was not independent of human purpose. Martin wanted to extend the humanist method to all of education, for traditional education as currently practiced had not done this. It had, to the contrary, destroyed intellectual freedom and perpetuated crowd thinking. How had traditional education done this? By divorcing thinking from doing. By treating knowledge as learning of isolated facts. By treating the act of learning as passive reception of information imposed by external sources. By teaching subjects as isolated 'things' apart from the world of experience, as systems of thought without reference to real problems. Traditional education accepted truth second hand from authority, and that was what Martin meant by crowd thinking. (23)

By 1926 Martin had developed fully his philosophy of liberal education applied to adults. The Meaning of Liberal Education was published in 1926, the same year that the Carnegie Corporation sponsored American Association for Adult Education was organized and Eduard Lindeman's The Meaning of Adult Education (24) was published. The organization of a national association and the publication of the first American interpretations of adult education indicated the coming of age of adult education as a movement, but these events also indicated the deep division among the theorists and institutional promoters about the nature and direction of the movement.

In the twenties adult education seemed to be everybody's interest and business, so much so that Martin called adult education a mass movement. The desire for knowledge was so intense and widespread that it could be compared with the mass hunger for learning in the thirteenth century. (25) The movement, however, lacked direction, Martin believed, and it had been used for many purposes that were not always educational. Some hailed adult education as the salvation of democracy, and others used adult education as an instrument of propaganda to achieve the ends of their various causes and agencies.

Adult education was an ancient practice, but it had to be adapted to conditions in the United States. In ancient Greece adults gathered around Socrates, Plato, and Aristotle and extended their education through life. The European universities of the thirteenth century were institutions for adult education, a place of residence for mature men and women to study. In the twenties in the United States adults did not have leisure as in Greece nor could they retreat to a cloistered environment. They had to combine education with a life of activity. Knowledge could not remain the property of professional educators. Adult education aimed not at making specialists out of lay persons but at making the 'cultivated amateur'. (26) 'I should like,' Martin said, 'to picture the liberally educated individual as a mellow amateur, competent and well-informed, but with all natural and human, wholly at ease with his knowledge and master of his technique; one whose thinking is plain and whose mind does not squeak as it runs along.' (27)

Martin wanted education to become culture outside the classroom, that is, to become a dominant interest that changed 'the tastes and habits of thought of the community'. (28) Education, however, had not become part of national life; professional knowledge had not been transferred to the daily lives of the people. Instead, they grounded their behavior in folkways, ancient dogmas, materialism, and 'newspaper-fashioned public opinion'. Only one way could lead out of this morass: make liberal education the aim of adult education.

With liberal education as the aim of adult education, adult educators could keep adult education from becoming standardized after the fashion of the public schools and from becoming the captives of slogans and special interests. As to serving slogans and special interests, the various types of adult education activities such as training labor leaders and farmers' institutes were important, but they were not education. As to the formal education system, Martin regarded adult education as a protest against this system and warned against placing adult education in the hands of public educators because their learning had stopped. As he put it: 'Their influence is everywhere to divert this mature interest in learning to the only ends such professional educators know; service to the state, conformity and routine, material advancement and industrial efficiency, the uplift of the masses.' (29)

Another reason for making liberal education the aim of adult education was to provide teachers with standards for working with adults. Martin recognized as did others that the methods of adult education had to differ from those for children. Adult learners were volunteers, and while they might lack knowledge they had experience to which the knowledge must be related. But the fact that adults were volunteer learners and had life experience did not change the aim of adult education. The aim must be focused on the question, 'What is the educated person?' Moreover, the aim was important for another reason. Students came to class with strong opinions, and to keep the students in class the instructor sometimes conceded to their prejudices. But the prejudices of students should not become the goal of the learning.

Openly elitist, Martin, nevertheless, believed that the common people had a natural desire for education; if given opportunity they might stumble on the meaning of liberal education. Adult education, however, was not something given to the masses and college education for those of privilege. Education was for everyone, and there was hope that some - including the college educated - might select for themselves the superior way.

This superior way manifested itself in four characteristics - attitudes and behaviors - of the liberally educated person. First, the educated person had gotten rid of his delusions, had formed his own opinions, was able to examine and weigh points of view, and no longer necessarily followed the crowd opinion. Second, the educated person made progress in his thinking by examining the presuppositions which underlay the arguments for specific points of view. Third, educated persons grew in freedom, in an atmosphere of tolerance where differences of opinion were accepted and then acted from self-discipline and not as part of the crowd. Fourth, liberal education led to an appreciation of human worth and to distinctions of worth.

To Martin, human progress occurred not through social movements but through the changes that persons made in their thinking and behavior each day. The basic problem stemmed from people getting caught in 'the delusion of infallibility'. As long as people failed to recognize that the products of their reason had become outmoded, they would be unable to accept the new challenges presented at each stage of their development. Liberal education for Martin was a philosophy of living. It involved winning a victory over one's own nature, of facing the things that one would not like to admit. Such education had no immediate or direct value. This kind of learning was valuable for its own sake, the worth was intrinsic. And no one should subject education to some ulterior end such as citizenship, efficiency, or emancipating the working class.

If liberal education was not to be subjected to ulterior ends, then it was clear that education could not be propaganda, book learning, or animal training. Martin acknowledged that in the twenties education was often confused with propaganda, but the educator and the propagandist had different goals. The propagandist was concerned with what people thought and attempted to get them to do something. The propagandist neither respected the personality of the person nor encouraged critical examination of issues. Teachers had the right to take a position on social issues as a citizen. But when the spirit of propaganda supplanted education, something insidious happened: authority replaced experimentation and commands to do replaced the awakening of curiosity.

As important as books were in liberal education, a liberal education was not book learning; it was never confused with getting an education, having degrees, or displaying knowledge. Reading did not substitute for living and reality. 'Education is the organization of knowledge into human excellence.' (30)

Education as training did not equip persons with the ability to reflect on knowledge and gain wisdom. Martin minced no words about his contempt for contemporary educational psychology: it was no more than animal training in which pedagogical principles were borrowed from animal psychology and the environment organized to bring about desired responses. A person's education became a set of conditioned responses, for this psychology assumed that insight was not part of learning. In Martin's judgment, animal learning - educational psychology - rested upon two wrong propositions. First, the metaphysical assumption equated the mind with what it had learned and made it a product of its environment. Second, education was a means to efficient service, a view growing out of present day industry that made work the end of human existence.

Education, however, could not be reduced to learning by doing. An individual might learn how to perform a task by repeated performances but would not learn the reason for learning the task or the relation of the task to broader issues of life. (31) Without mentioning Edward Thorndike by name, Martin criticized a report of Thorndike's research on adult learning ability for equating the problem of adult education with facility in acquiring new habits. Thorndike found the age at which the maximum speed in habit formation occurred to be between 18 and 24. Thorndike's approach to adult learning violated Martin's deepest convictions about education: habit formation as learning process based on animal psychology made the learner an automoton who acquired habits but no insights.

If animal psychology as learning theory for adults was psychology misapplied, then workers' education was the prime example of adult education misguided. Martin challenged the position that the education required for persons who work differed from other educated people and that it should be addressed to non-educational ends. Such advocates based this view on several misconceptions. One misconception was that education for workers had a socially conserving influence: better informed workers would be more sympathetic to employers and more content with their status in the economic structure.

In a second misconception work was regarded as the genuine method of education, based on the belief that one learns in relation to the real things of life. Martin did not regard experience as the best teacher. Experience taught only what was experienced, but without reflection people were not any wiser.

A third misconception claimed that education was the tool of the vested interests to keep the working class in place. The argument followed that workers must have their own education for the 'class struggle'. The aim of workers' education should then be to free labor from the domination of capital and enable labor to gain control of industrial society. Martin equated this position with radical propaganda.

With regard to this radical position, Martin admitted for the sake of argument that 'traditional education is class education, elaborated in the interest of the dominant elements in society'. (32) But he argued that traditional education could have a function other than 'systematic exploitation'. It could improve the use of leisure, aid in discriminating between ends worthy of efforts and those that were not, and aid in the development of personality. In the past, these were the possession of the few; now they could be the possession of the many.

These interests, Martin argued, were not those of any particular class. Liberal education was for persons because they were human and not because they were workers. To those who envisioned a new civilization arising in the laboring classes in which new ideals and standards were expressed in a 'working class ideology', Martin could only disagree. (33) The working class did not have a culture apart from the rest of America. They participated in the same activities, dressed alike, bought cars, and read popular journals. They, in short, acted like the middle class.

Educated persons responded to the common world - to the same situation as uneducated persons - but with a different set of values. 'Education is not so much a special interest separated from other interests as it is a method for transforming all our interests.' (34)

In 1928, Martin published his most balanced, comprehensive, and non-invective analysis of education and contemporary social conditions in Charles A. Beard's Whither Mankind: A Panorama of Modern Civilization. (35) Beard asked leading authorities to write chapters on 'several phases of modern civilization', including science, business, labor, law and government, war and peace, health, the family, and play.

What function education should perform in this modern world characterized by industrialization and urbanization could not have been foreseen by the formulators of the classical tradition. Its function had not been understood by modern day persons who saw education as social service, specialization, vocational training, habit formation, or preparation for citizenship. The education then evolving to equip persons for the emerging technology and the classical tradition were both inadequate. There could be no retreat to the classical tradition for it had lost its vitality, had become mere formalism. The classics were read without regard to the experimental attitude that permeated them, and the scholastic spirit with its emphasis on drill and examination had become part of education. The classical tradition had become the 'genteel tradition', but 'a genteel tradition aloof from contemporary reality' was not an education appropriate for the machine age.

The education needed in this new period could not ignore the present as did the classicists nor could it ignore the past as did many moderns. It had to combine both. A living culture had continuity that included both the present and the past. Education could not be dismembered into the 'practical' and the 'cultural'. The new education had two tasks. On the one hand, education had to provide understanding of the modern world, of the machine age produced by natural science and industry. On the other, education was to help men reflect on the directions and ends which they were pursuing so that they would have 'the ability to take a philosophical attitude toward experience'. (36)

Martin, unfortunately, was unable to keep both these tasks before him, for he retreated into the world of the 'cultural'. In his desire to make liberal education a philosophy of living and to promote excellence as the goal of adult education, he achieved what he had feared. Liberal education, as he envisioned it, became a 'cult or faction of the adult education movement in America'. His vision was simply too narrow.

NOTES

1.   Everett Dean Martin, 'A Free Man's Education', Adult Education and Democracy, (American Association for Adult Education, NY, 1936), p.13.

2.   For my understanding of the People's Institute in this section, I have drawn extensively from Robert B. Fisher, The People's Institute of New York City, 1897-1934: Culture, Progressive Democracy, and the People, Ph.D. Dissertation, New York University, 1974.

3.   Ibid., pp.23-31.

4.   Ibid., pp.424-6.

5.   Everett Dean Martin, The Behavior of Crowds: A Psychological Study, (Harper and Brothers, NY, 1920).

6.   David Spitz, Patterns of Anti-Democratic Thought, rev. ed., (The Free Press, NY, 1965), pp. 124, 127, 129; Rush Welter, Popular Education and Democratic Thought in America, (Columbia University Press, NY, 1962), p.305.

7.   Everett Dean Martin, Civilizing Ourselves: Intellectual Maturity in the Modern World, (W.W. Norton,

NY, 1932).
8. Ibid., p.20.
9. Ibid., pp.10-13.
10. Ibid., p.84.
11. Ibid., pp.283-4.
12. Ibid., p.184.
13. Everett Dean Martin, The Conflict of the Individual and the Mass in the Modern World, (Henry Holt and Company, NY, 1932), p.175.
14. Ibid., p.159.
15. Everett Dean Martin, Liberty, (W.W. Norton, NY, 1930), pp.246-53.
16. Martin, Conflict, p.178.
17. Martin, Civilizing Ourselves, p.266.
18. Martin, Liberty, pp.5-10.
19. Ibid.
20. Martin, Behavior, p.281, (italics in original).
21. Ibid., p.290.
22. Ibid., pp.282-3.
23. Ibid., pp.287-93.
24. Everett Dean Martin, The Meaning of Liberal Education, (W.W. Norton, NY, 1926).
25. Ibid., p.2.
26. Ibid., p.309.
27. Ibid., p.66.
28. Ibid., p.310.
29. Ibid., p.316.
30. Ibid., p.70.
31. Ibid., pp.36-43.
32. Ibid., p.175.
33. Ibid., p.177.
34. Ibid., pp.160-1.
35. Everett Dean Martin, 'Education', in Charles A. Beard, (ed.), Whither Mankind: A Panorama of Modern Civilization, (Longmans, Green & Company, NY, 1928), pp.354-86.
36. Ibid., p.368.

Chapter Five

ROBERT HUTCHINS, MORTIMER ADLER AND 'LIBERAL EDUCATION BEYOND SCHOOLING' THROUGH THE GREAT BOOKS

In the fifties the Great Books program of adult liberal education swept across the nation, attracting attention, enlisting a large number of participants, and evoking controversy. Robert M. Hutchins and Mortimer J. Adler of the University of Chicago, the founders of the program, had definite ideas about the aims of education at all levels, and they clearly wanted educational reform along the lines of classical liberal education. But neither Hutchins nor Adler could claim to be originator of this approach to education. John Erskine at Columbia University had tested the 'great books' undergraduate course, and Everett Dean Martin at the People's Institute adapted the course for adults studying in community settings.

THE ORIGIN OF THE GREAT BOOKS

John Erskine, Professor of English, initiated his General Honors course at Columbia University in 1921. He first presented his ideas about liberal education in a paper called 'The Moral Obligation to Be Intelligent'. He taught a course similar to the Honors Course to service men in Europe where he worked in World War I with the Army-YMCA educational project and later as administrator of the Army Educational Commission.

Erskine's General Honors course was one of two efforts at Columbia after the war for general education. Faculty concern for general education was expressed during World War I with a course on 'War Issues' to study the underlying causes of the war. In 1919 the course, revised and titled

'Contemporary Civilization', was offered by the departments of history, economics, government, and philosophy. (1) Many of the faculty believed that the demise of classical education and the rise of specialization in narrow fields of study had left confusion about common ideas and shared standards of judgment.

Erskine's ideas for the General Honors Course on the 'Classics of Western Thought' were novel. A professor of English, he nevertheless believed that every educated person had competence to lead discussions about great books. Erskine divided this first class in 1921 into two groups, each met on Wednesday evening, and at each session the students discussed one book which they had read that week. Erskine's colleagues thought it impossible to read and master a book a week. Erskine replied that the great books were written for the general public, not specialists, they were popular, and the people read them quickly, without waiting for someone to interpret them. (2)

After the first year, Erskine expected the students to have acquired much information, formed ideas about literature and life, and developed esthetic emotions, which they would share in common. 'This store of information,' Erskine believed, 'would be the true scholarly and cultural basis for human understanding and communication.'

The General Honors Course was open to juniors and seniors, and Mortimer J. Adler, a member of the junior class, applied and was accepted. After graduation, Adler accepted a faculty appointment as instructor and became a discussion leader. In 1923 several new Honors sections were formed and two instructors with competence in different areas were assigned to each section. Adler was paired with Mark Van Doren in English.

In 1926 Adler began work in the adult education program at the People's Institute. In that year the Institute co-operated with Columbia University and the American Association for Adult Education to adapt the general honors course to adult learners. Adler and other members of the general honors faculty served as the discussion leaders. (3) Scott Buchanan, then Assistant Director of the People's Institute, invited Adler to try his hand at public lecturing. In March and April, 1926, Adler gave eight lectures on methods of psychology at the Manhattan Trade School on New York's lower East Side. When Buchanan went to the University of Virginia, Adler became the Assistant Director to Everett Dean Martin. As part of his duties he lectured at community sites and at the Great Hall of the Cooper Union. At the Tuesday and Sunday lectures at the Great Hall, the Assistant Director served as chairman, introducing the speaker and repeating the questions during the forum.

HUTCHINS' EDUCATION AND THE COUNTERATTACK AGAINST SCIENTIFIC NATURALISM

It was fortuitous that Adler and Hutchins became acquainted. Adler, at Columbia, and Hutchins, Dean of the Yale Law School, were both conducting projects on the law of evidence. C.K. Ogden, a publisher, was visiting Hutchins and told him of Adler - a young psychologist, logician, and philosopher - and his project on the law of evidence. Hutchins invited Adler to New Haven to visit. They then collaborated on a law of evidence project, beginning a friendship and collaborative relationship that was to last a lifetime. (4)

Robert Hutchins had become a member of the law faculty at Yale University at 26. In his career at Yale as professor of the law of evidence and Dean of the Law School, Hutchins was a legal empiricist: the law was what the courts did, not an 'unchanging, self-evident reality'. (5) As dean he worked to increase the emphasis of the empirical and social sciences in the curriculum and to promote collaboration of the law and medical faculties with the social science faculty.

Hutchins began to doubt legal realism, especially as he began to explore the law of evidence, supposedly based on psychology and logic. (6) Later Hutchins would claim that at this time he began to recognize his lack of 'education'. His opportunity to remedy that lack soon came. In late April of 1929, Hutchins, then 30, was appointed President of the University of Chicago. Adler sent a telegram of congratulations and shortly after proposed that Hutchins appoint him to the philosophy department.

In October of 1929 after Hutchins had already moved to Chicago, Adler and Hutchins met in New York City. That proved to be a fateful meeting: the seeds were planted that soon germinated into the University of Chicago curriculum reform and the Great Books program. Hutchins told Adler that he had not thought much about education, and Adler confessed that he had not either. Adler described the General Honors Course at Columbia with Erskine and called reading the great books his best educational experience. (7) Adler called this experience 'a college in itself - the whole of a liberal education or certainly the core of it'. (8) Hutchins himself had not read many of these books. (9)

After Hutchins' inauguration in November of 1929, he secured an appointment for Adler as associate professor of philosophy. In early 1930 Hutchins communicated to Adler his proposal to become an 'educated man'. He asked Adler to co-teach a General Honors Course with him the following September. They would select a group of entering freshmen and carry them through the sophomore year on a model of the Columbia program. This program would be the opening effort in curriculum reform and the beginning of Hutchins' education. (10) In an address entitled 'The Autobiography of an Uneducated Man', Hutchins claimed that his education began at 32 when he began to teach the Great Books with Mortimer Adler. (11)

At Chicago Hutchins abandoned the realist approach for a neo-Aristotelian metaphysics. Purcell claims that Hutchins' move toward metaphysics was his personal answer to his intellectual problems. But Hutchins was not alone in this struggle to find first principles and the unity of knowledge; many others rejected the scientific orientation. At Chicago Hutchins began to examine education as a whole. He came to Chicago believing in the goal of education to be a thorough understanding of human activities. (12) Hutchins first indicated his new synthesis in 'The University of Utopia', an article written in March, 1931.

It was in a Convocation at the University of Chicago in December, 1933, that Hutchins presented his critique about the university as presently structured. For 300 years society had placed great faith in the accumulation of facts, but this hope had not been realized. Science had been confused with information, ideas with facts, and knowledge with data. Hutchins did not deny the importance of accumulating facts through observation and experimentation. But modern empirical science had come to be mainly experiment and measurement - an application of mathematics to experience - and social studies and the humanities had been influenced by the natural sciences.

The university had become the place of specialists focusing on research instead of grappling with fundamentals. Their efforts failed to give direction to modern life because reason had been absent. Hutchins knew the remedy: make the university 'a center of rational thought', a place 'to grapple with those fundamental principles which rational thought seeks to establish'. (13)

In 1935 Hutchins presented his fully developed ideas about the basic principles of general education in the Storr Lectures at Yale University, published in 1936 as The Higher Learning in America. (14) Only one remedy would suffice: re-establish general education. The elective system, vocational training and education by current events had proven to be inadequate substitutes for the 'permanent studies' that treated what was common for humanity. (15)

Hutchins wanted to find principles around which the university faculty could find unity. He wanted also to provide the specialists in the university 'a common stock of fundamental ideas' that permit them to communicate with one another outside their areas of expertise. The medieval university had a principle of unity in theology, but this was not possible for the contemporary university. The Greeks provided to Hutchins the clue: metaphysics was the ordering principle, the highest science because it sought the cause of things. Hutchins never explained what he meant by metaphysics or how the university could organize itself around such a concept.

He was clear about his belief that intellectual development was the only role of higher education. Human nature had common elements that were the same at any time or place, and Hutchins could not conceive of 'educating a man to live in any particular time or place, to adjust him to any particular environment'.

EDUCATION OUTSIDE THE UNIVERSITY

Other forms of education were important and necessary, but Hutchins wanted the university to stop appropriating to itself the educational work that belonged to other institutions. All education was not formal education, and formal education alone could not be responsible for developing fully the individual. (16) The home, church, the state, the newspapers, the radio, the movies, and the neighborhood club provided experiences for youth that the university could not provide and should not. Adults who spent none of their time in school were or should be growing in wisdom. In the course of their daily lives, adults had experiences which they would be able to understand and assimilate if they had learned to reason when they were being educated.

In the thirties, prior to adapting the great books discussion approach with adult groups, Hutchins had given attention to broader issues about adult education. (17) He was not naive about the constraints that impeded the freedom of leaders who took adult education in directions independent of what he called the ruling class. Hutchins emphasized this reality in an address to the Employed Officers Association of the YMCA in 1933 when the 'Y' struggled for financial resources. The professional leadership of the 'Y' - the 'Y' secretaries - had to constantly direct the public and the board of trustees away from property and money to the real function of the 'Y', its program. Secretaries could not work toward their professional ideals if they had to be concerned about how acceptable their program ideas were to the business community and the 'ruling class'. To implement programs that incorporated 'Y' values, the 'Y' secretaries must have freedom in the same way a university professor had freedom to express unpopular views based on research. Because the forces that made up public opinion in the United States were selfish and not Christian in any sense, such a program could be carried out only if the professional leadership could be guaranteed security and the organization declared its independence.

To the 'Y' secretaries, Hutchins called adult education 'the most complicated problem in the whole education field'. In 1935 before the Pittsburgh Teachers Association, he said that the task now before the country was 'the tutelage of the entire population'. This task included adult education, a 'field from which we have long withheld our blessing'. The neglect stemmed, partly, because adult education had been thought of 'as the foible of the philanthropist and the social worker', and not as education. It meant lectures by persons who wanted to change the social order in some way that most other persons found disagreeable. Adult education had also been neglected bcause of preoccupation with children and youth, but this neglect did not obscure its importance. Hutchins recognized that the education of adults must be undertaken 'although the field is uncharted and our experience is almost nil'.

After the depression, Hutchins projected that Americans would have more leisure time because of a shorter work day and week. They would not be content,

Hutchins said, with sleeping, watching movies, and driving on the highway; they would want more stimulating activities such as adult education. But adult education was in an experimental stage, and professional educators who were used to thinking about institutions and curricula could hinder this experiment. The most rewarding aspects of adult education were more like extra-curricular activities than organized instruction. In adult education, the school should operate as a 'center of community life, reflecting the community's interest in music, art, the drama, and current affairs ...' (18)

GREAT BOOKS FOR ADULTS

Shortly after Hutchins and Adler began the General Honors course at Chicago, university alumni in Highland Park, Illinois, asked Adler to conduct a Great Books discussion group for them. The Highland Park Great Books group lasted for 15 years. Though successful, this experiment with college graduates was an isolated incident. But in 1940 Adler introduced the Great Books to the general public with the publication of How To Read A Book. (19)

The rules and recommendations in How To Read A Book grew out of a course that Adler began in 1934-35 for pre-law students to provide them with a background in the humanities and training in the liberal arts of reading, writing, listening, and speaking. He first formulated his ideas on reading for the general reader in 1938 when asked to address a group during alumni week. Drawing on his experience in conducting great books discussions, he lectured on the art of reading, and the lecture was later transcribed and published in the Chicago Alumni News. Adler gave the lecture several times.

Because he needed money, he proposed to his long-time friend, Clifton Fadiman, then editor-in-chief at Simon and Schuster, a book on the topic. Adler wrote the book in July, 1939, writing a chapter a day for 17 consecutive days. This was not Adler's first or last book, but it proved to be his most successful one. (20) Adler wrote How To Read A Book for the average reader and for adults who had become aware of how little they had gotten out of their schooling. Education did not stop with schooling, so Adler admonished his readers, and their educational fate did not rest with the school system.

Adults who continued their education through reading would have to work hard because reading was a complex activity. Adler intended his prescription for reading a book to make this complex process manageable. The reader first had to identify the type of book; one read expository works differently than imaginative literature. The reader should read the book three times: first, structurally and analytically to understand what was in the book, second, interpretively and synthetically, and third, critically or evaluatively to assess the book's worth.

Adler intended more than just helping adults read better; he wanted adults - as the book's subtitle indicated - to learn 'the art of getting a liberal education'. The Great Books, he advocated, provided the best way of getting a liberal education, and Adler drew up a list of over 130 authors. Their works were the curriculum of adult education. These authors addressed issues that were contemporary, and Adler demonstrated how by reading several authors on the same topic the reader could join in their 'Great Conversation'.

In 1939 the University College of the University of Chicago began offering Great Books seminars to the general public but with not much success. The real turning point came in 1942-43 with the organization of a seminar for adults at the University Club in Chicago. Hutchins asked Wilbur Munnecke, a university vice-president and former executive at Marshall Fields, about organizing an executive training program for business students. To this Munnecke replied that persons who were already executives really needed the program to help them read and write. (21) Another group might also benefit from such a seminar, Munnecke suggested: trustees of the University who did not understand Hutchins' reform efforts. (22)

Thirty businessmen, industrialists, bankers, lawyers, and their wives were invited to the first class meeting on 27 October 1943. Hutchins and Adler moderated. The class subsequently met every two weeks and gained the attention of prominent Chicago capitalists. Calling themselves 'The Fat Man's Class', the group caught the attention of the public, generated favorable press coverage, and increased applications to the University College. The demand, however, exceeded the capacity of the University College. The idea that later became the Great Books Foundation began to germinate.

In 1944 Cyril Houle became the administrator of the

University College and chaired a governing committee of which Adler was a member. At a meeting, someone raised the question of using people with no prior teaching experience as moderators of the discussion groups. Adler agreed and thought that they might even be less pedantic than professionals if they were trained in the Socratic method. The Head of the Chicago Public Library offered to help by enlisting librarians and others in a training course. Adler prepared a series of talks about the great books and how to lead discussions. He held ten sample great books discussions to demonstrate the method. The University College and the Chicago Public Library then organized great books discussion clubs and used these trained leaders. The experiment was successful. A revised and expanded version of Adler's talks was published as A Manual for Great Books Discussion Leaders. Between 1945 and 1947, Adler travelled across the country as a missionary for the great books.

In 1947 Robert Hutchins and William Benton, with assistance from the University of Chicago and foundations, organized the Great Books Foundation. The Great Books Foundation sold paperback reprints of the great books, trained great books leaders, organized discussion groups, and published training manuals. In a year, 7,000 adults in Chicago had enrolled in seminars organized by the Great Books Foundation, and less than a year later over 43,000 persons in 300 cities were members of great books clubs. The Mayor of Chicago proclaimed the week of 25 September 1948, 'Great Books Week'. Adler gave several addresses and conducted with Hutchins a discussion of Plato's dialogue on the trial of Socrates before a capacity crowd in Orchestra Hall. Other public demonstrations were held in Milwaukee and Los Angeles. In 1950, the National Broadcasting Company, which carried the University of Chicago's Round Table, featured a conversation between Adler and Clare Boothe Luce on the great books.

Before the organization of the Great Books Foundation in 1947, plans were underway for the publication project that in 1952 appeared as the Great Books of the Western World. In 1943 the Encyclopaedia Britannica which had been owned by Sears, Roebuck and Company since 1920 except for a short interval was offered to the University of Chicago. The University became owner of the preferred stock and William Benton became owner of the common stock and head of the publishing company. Benton and Hutchins had been classmates at Yale, and in 1935 Benton, after a successful career in advertising, came to the University as a public relations advisor to Hutchins. Benton created a Board of Editors and made Hutchins the chair, a position he held until 1974 when Adler succeeded him.

Less than six months after Benton became head, he proposed a new publishing venture. A member of the University College Great Books Club, he had been unable to purchase conveniently the assigned readings. In a meeting with Hutchins and Adler, Benton proposed the possibility of editing a set of the great books. Hutchins opposed the idea unless some way could be found to make the books useful for individual use without the aid of discussion groups.

Adler set out to find a way to make the great books an instrument of self-education, and in the summer of 1943 he found the answer while working on How To Think About War and Peace. Turning to the great books for the authors' views about war and peace, he found many passages he had not marked or noticed. It occurred to him that the great books could become meaningful if persons read them over and over with a specific question in mind. Constructing an index would make the books educational and not just a commercial venture. Adler's proposal for an idea-index was approved, but its completion proved to be difficult, requiring seven years and a budget of almost one million dollars.

An advisory board of editors formed of persons who had been closely associated with the great books - Scott Buchanan, Stringfellow Barr, Mark Van Doren, Joseph Schwab, Clarence Faust, John Erskine, and Alexander Meiklejohn - drew up several lists of the great books before selecting 443 works by 74 authors. In 1952 a 54 volume set was published containing Hutchins' essay, two volumes for the idea-index called 'The Great Ideas: A Syntopicon', and the 443 works by the 74 authors. This publication event occurred at the peak of the great books movement which flourished in the fifties and sixties before declining. (23)

A RATIONALE FOR THE USE OF THE GREAT BOOKS FOR THE LIBERAL EDUCATION FOR ADULTS

The rationale that Hutchins and Adler articulated for the use of the Great Books for the liberal education of adults was first developed in justifying the undergraduate reform at the University of Chicago. As they began to promote the Great Books for adults they expanded these ideas and tied them more specifically to adult education.

In his introductory essay to the Great Books of the Western World, Hutchins posed for him the central question: 'Do science, technology, industrialization, and specialization render the Great Conversation irrelevant?' (24) Until 50 years ago, the liberal arts and the Great Books stood as the center of education, but they had been displaced. Teachers of the classics had lost sight of their liberal values. Advocates of new modes of economic thought and knowledge production emerged who viewed experimental science as the only valid means of knowledge: only what could be counted could be justified as trustworthy knowledge. Unfortunately, too many theorists and practitioners in the disciplines of history, philosophy, and the social sciences tried to model their work to conform to patterns being used in the natural sciences.

New emphases in education that resulted from science, technology, industrialization, and specialization displaced the liberal arts, but that did not render the Great Conversation irrelevant. To Hutchins, liberal education remained as the education for everyone. Without liberal education, a community could not be created. A community required communication, and communication required common language, common ideas, and common human standards. Creating a community could not be separated from a common education. If a common education was impossible, then so was community. The training of specialists had emphasized the way that persons were different, but the present world crisis required an education for those aspects of men and women that were the same. 'The West needs,' Hutchins said, 'an education that draws out our common humanity rather than our individuality.' (25)

The same science, technology, industrialization, and specialization that made liberal education appear irrelevant had also made liberal education possible for all by the leisure it gave to the common people. The possibility of liberal education for all hinged upon economic and political conditions that Adler believed were being realized in the United States after World War II. The distinction between a working class and a leisure class had begun to disappear and universal suffrage had abolished the distinction between a ruling class and subject class. Everyone - not just the exceptional few - must be educated for a life of citizenship. Adler argued that a truly classless society would evolve if the trend continued: 'a politically classless society in which all men are citizens and members of the ruling class; and an economically classless society in which all men are capitalists and members of the leisure class'. (26)

Few would agree that the United States has become such a society, but a society in which free men with leisure pursued liberal education had been briefly realized in Athenian Greece, and Hutchins and Adler turned often to this ancient example for inspiration. When their opponents pointed out that this education was aristocratic, Hutchins replied that in Athenian Greece it was the education of those who had leisure and political power. Now all men and women had leisure because of technology and machines, and all had political power because of democracy. Liberal education's original association with undemocratic ideals in the past did not invalidate it. (27)

In the Preface to The Great Conversation, Hutchins acknowledged elements of novelty in presenting the Great Books as the key ingredient in liberal education for adults. The Great Books had almost disappeared from American education in the past 50 years. Hutchins called this disappearance an aberration, not progress, and restoring the Great Books simply continued a tradition that had been interrupted. Restoring books to the education of adults ran counter to the old conception of adult education as compensatory and to contemporary forms of adult education as job training. Education was to be lifelong and books should play the central role.

Why the Great Books? Hutchins argued that the Great Books of the Western world constituted the Great Conversation. (28) The books selected as the Great Books were those believed indispensable to a liberal education because of their merit and their representation of a particular period, epoch, or point of view. They contained both truth and error. The books included covered 25 centuries, ending with the nineteenth century except for some of Freud's books. While the Great Conversation did not end with the nineteenth century, the advisory board felt it could not judge the great books of the twentieth century.

In How To Read a Book, Adler called the Great Books 'original communications', and he believed that a great book had six signs.

(a) They were widely read and had accumulated an audience.
(b) They were popular, written for a popular audience and

intended for beginners, not specialists.

(c) They were always contemporary and never outmoded by changing schools of thought. Rather than a record of a dead civilization, they were 'the most potent civilizing forces in the world today' (29) because they treated fundamental human problems that did not change.

(d) They were the most readable, the best written books, the masterpieces of the liberal arts, and could be read at different levels of interpretation.

(e) They were the most instructive and enlightening of all books. Adler called them the 'primary teachers' of mankind because they were original communications.

(f) They dealt with the most significant and unsolved problems of human life. (30)

Because these books treated problems of human life, they were - even as classics - not removed from concerns of ordinary people in their daily lives. The Great Books could be read for themes of daily conversation that persons got from the radio and newspapers and talk about to their friends. (31) In an instructive section, Adler showed the reader how to move from topics in the popular media, then to the themes treated in the better contemporary books to the Great Books, then to see how the Great Books treated the themes. Contemporary writers drew their major ideas from a few sources, mainly authors of the Great Books. By reading the Great Books from the past, beginning with the earliest written and moving to the present, readers would understand the later authors because the readers would have read the books the author had read. The books should also be read in relation to another book or books. Adler calls this 'extrinsic reading': books read in light of other books.

The Great Books provided the sources for engaging in this Great Conversation with the best minds about enduring human problems. The books were to be studied from a particular perspective: the humanistic approach to learning. The humanistic approach examined the permanent aspects of the subject matter - the constancy of human nature - and 'the universal and abiding principles, the fundamental ideas and insights, the controlling canons of procedure or method ...' (32) Instead of seeking mastery of the subject, humanistic study cultivated the liberal skills. Liberal education, Hutchins noted, consisted 'in the recognition of basic problems, in knowledge of distinctions and interrelations in subject matter, and in the comprehension of ideas'. (33)

The liberally educated person could operate in all fields of thought as a generalist, understand what was important in any field, and relate that to the field in which he was a specialist. The methods of liberal education were the liberal arts, and liberal education resulted in discipline in the liberal arts: ability to 'read, write, speak, listen, understand, and think'. It was discipline in the liberal arts that made learning through the lifespan possible. As Adler noted in his autobiography, liberally educated persons had competence as learners which they could use for lifetime learning as one of the creative pursuits of leisure. This kind of education was possible for all persons, no matter how intellectually endowed.

In How To Read A Book, Adler called liberal education 'democracy's strongest bulwark': only men with free minds were free men. (34) That freedom had its source in discipline, in the discipline of the mind. The mind could be disciplined, Adler believed, by reading, listening, and talking. Reading developed analytical and critical powers, and the mind trained to discuss had these powers sharpened. Ability to deal with arguments made persons more tolerant and patient and checked the animal impulse to impose their opinions on others. To Adler, the only authority was reason, and only a trained intelligence could live the life of reason.

HOW EDUCATION DIFFERS FROM SCHOOLING AND HOW ADULTS DIFFER FROM CHILDREN

As early as 1940 in How To Read A Book Adler had spoken out against the misconception of adult education as remedial schooling or as avocational pursuits. This misconception resulted from confusing schooling with education. (35) Schooling had to do with habit formation and training for persons - usually children - under institutional care, protected from the consequences of their own behavior.

Education, in contrast, referred to learning by mature men and women who had matured because of their experiences in the activities of adult life with work and family. Maturity came from aging, from living, in which one experienced pain, suffering, and grief. Because children had not had those experiences associated with aging, they were not mature and thus not educable. Education consisted of growth in understanding, insight, and wisdom, and these ideas required experience to take root. Because of these experiences, adults could think better and learn better than children in the sense of cultivating their minds.

In making this judgment, Adler worked with philosophical categories, not with empirical evidence. While he did not dismiss Edward Thorndike's research as unimportant, he refused to base the liberal education position on the validity of those findings. As he pointed out, Thorndike's experiments in adult learning presented scientific evidence on the ability of adults to learn, but this belief had been held throughout Western civilization. Plato's Republic laid out a scheme of learning through the life span, and Aristotle's Ethics pointed out that the young could not learn ethical principles because they were immature.

A false belief permeated education at all levels: education must be play and learning should not be painful. (36) This idea pervaded schooling, colleges, and even adult education. Persons who graduated from such schools entered adult life without preparation for carrying out self-directed education: they were unwilling to suffer the pain of learning. Adler called the various agencies of adult education 'soft-minded' about the public they serve. In a telling description about how these agencies baby the public, Adler said: 'They have turned the whole nation - so far as education is concerned - into a kindergarten.' (37) In other areas of adult life a person succeeded by hard work. Why should adult education be an exception to the rule of life?

Adler objected to the conception of education as external and additive; this reduced education to the acquisition of information. Not so said Adler: 'education is an interior transformation of a person's mind and character'. The adult was 'plastic material' to be transformed by what was good for the adult and not just by his own inclination. The transformation, however, could only be effected by the adult's own activity: intellectual activity. The adult learner had to be challenged. They learned when the material was over their heads; good education did not just take people where they were and left them there. Adler had found his model of education at the People's Institute under Everett Dean Martin, describing it as 'the best adult education that has existed in this country'.

Adult education was not just childhood education 'writ large,' for the two levels were clearly distinguishable. First, because adults were responsible for their lives, adult education was always voluntary. Only children could be compelled to go to school. Second, in education at the adult level all participants were equal. Adult learning situations did not have a teacher in the sense of the teacher's superiority to students because adult education entailed mature human beings talking to one another. Third, education in adult life was interminable. Because the goal of education was wisdom, the process must go on for the whole life. Because the mind was a living thing, it must be constantly fed to stay alive. (38)

Schooling for children and youth and education for adults differed, but Adler did not denigrate the importance of schooling. In fact, he emphasized its importance and reinterpreted its mission in light of adult education. What should the schools do for the young? he asked. The schools could not educate. No graduate of schools, not even of universities, graduated as an educated person. But the beginning of the educated person began in schooling with the discipline children received in the liberal arts: the ability to read, write, speak, and think. In school they should experience intellectual stimulation and be enticed by learning itself so that they would continue to learn after leaving school. Schools could give 'the skills of learning and the wish to learn, so that in adult life they will want to go on learning and will have the skills to use in the process'. The young should leave schooling as competent learners, prepared and inspired to continue their learning in formal higher education, in other agencies, and by self-directed means.

Hutchins and Adler gave an unequivocal but limited answer to the issue of a unifying principle for adult education. Their idea of humanistic education has a broader and more compelling appeal than the means with which they proposed to achieve it.

NOTES

1. Carol S. Gruber, Mars and Minerva: World War I and the Uses of the Higher Learning in America, (Louisiana State University, Baton Rouge, LA, 1975), pp.312-38.
2. John Erskine, The Memory of Certain Persons, (J.B. Lippinncott Company, Philadelphia, PA, 1947), pp.342-3.

3.   Phillip Youtz, 'Experimental Classes in Adult Education', School and Society, 28, (July 28, 1928), pp.91-7.

4.   Mortimer Adler, Philosopher at Large: An Intellectual Autobiography, (Macmillan, NY, 1977), pp.107-8.

5.   These are the words of Edward A. Purcell, Jr., The Crisis of Democratic Theory: Scientific Naturalism and the Problem of Value, (The University Press of Kentucky, Lexington, 1973), p.140.

6.   Ibid., p.142.

7.   Adler, Philosopher, pp.128-9.

8.   Ibid., p.30.

9.   Robert Hutchins, Education for Freedom, (Louisiana State University Press, Baton Rouge, LA, 1943), p.13.

10.   Adler, Philosopher, p.126.

11.   Hutchins, Education, p.13.

12.   Purcell, The Crisis of Democratic Theory, p.142.

13.   Robert Hutchins, No Friendly Voice, (University of Chicago, Chicago, IL, 1936), p.27.

14.   Robert Hutchins, The Higher Learning in America, (Yale University Press, New Haven, CT, 1936).

15.   Ibid., pp.73-4.

16.   Ibid., p.68.

17.   Hutchins, No Friendly Voice, pp.95-114, 132-9.

18.   Ibid., p.113.

19.   Mortimer J. Adler, How To Read a Book: The Art of Getting a Liberal Education, (Simon and Schuster, NY, 1940).

20.   Adler, Philosopher, pp.201-5.

21.   James Sloan Allen, The Romance of Commerce and Culture: Capitalism, Modernism, and the Chicago-Aspen Crusade for Cultural Reform, (The University of Chicago Press, Chicago, IL, 1983), pp.104-6. Allen's book is the most comprehensive and critical account of the Great Books Movement.

22.   Adler, Philosopher, p.230.

23.   Ibid., p.228.

24.   Robert Hutchins, The Great Conversation: The Substance of a Liberal Education, (Encyclopedia Britannica, Chicago, IL, 1952), p.29.

25.   Ibid., p.50-1.

26.   Mortimer Adler, Reforming Education: The Schooling of a People and Their Education Beyond Schooling, (Westview Press, Boulder, CO, 1977), pp.128-9.

27. Hutchins, The Great Conversation, pp.xiv-xvi.
28. Ibid., pp.xvi-xxi.
29. Adler, How to Read, p.332.
30. Ibid., pp.328-38.
31. Ibid., pp.338-51.
32. Adler, Reforming Education, pp.161-2.
33. Hutchins, The Great Conversation, p.3.
34. Adler, How to Read, p.357.
35. Adler, Reforming Education, pp.241-55.
36. Ibid., pp.275-82.
37. Ibid., p.276.
38. Ibid., p.249-52.

Chapter Six

ALEXANDER MEIKLEJOHN AND JOHN WALKER POWELL ON LIBERAL EDUCATION AND THE STUDY OF CONTEMPORARY SOCIETY

Advocates of liberal education for adults are often characterized as being concerned solely about the intellectual development of individuals to the exclusion of social change. The positions of Everett Dean Martin, Mortimer Adler, and Robert Hutchins provide ample evidence for this judgment. The case of Alexander Meiklejohn (1872-1964) and his younger colleague, John Walker Powell (1904-), illustrates the gross oversimplification of this characterization. They had a broader agenda.

FORMING A PHILOSOPHY OF LIBERAL EDUCATION

Clues to Meiklejohn's views of liberal education and social change can be traced to his childhood. Born on February 3, 1872, in Rochdale, England, Meiklejohn moved with his family to Pawtucket, Rhode Island, in 1880. The consumer co-operative movement, to which Meiklejohn's family belonged, began in Rochdale, England in 1844. This movement profoundly influenced Meiklejohn, for he believed in some form of co-operative ownership all of his life and often criticized capitalism for the competitive way of life it fostered. (1) Social criticism and social action were legitimate, even necessary, aims of liberal education.

Trained in philosophy at Brown University and Cornell, Meiklejohn returned in 1907 to Brown as an instructor in philosophy and was later appointed dean, a deanship notable for promotion of student freedom and control. In 1911 Meiklejohn, then 40, became president at Amherst, serving until 1923 when he resigned at the request of the Board of Trustees. In shaping Amherst to conform to his image of a liberal college, Meiklejohn was strong-willed and opposed several traditions. He opposed the elective curriculum, and he wanted students to think and apply knowledge to life situations. To achieve this goal, he started a freshman class in 'Social and Economic Institutions' to study social complexity and the scope of conflicts and values in the United States. Unlike President Nicholas Murray Butler at Columbia University, Meiklejohn did not believe the war was necessary. Also unlike Butler, he opposed preparedness training on campus and insisted that all viewpoints about the war be presented to students.

At Amherst, Meiklejohn became involved in adult education. Believing that students and faculty should not be isolated in an academic cloister, he reached out into the community and collaborated with labor unions in establishing classes for workers in the mills at Holyoke and Springfield. Students and faculty taught courses in economics, history, government, reading, and writing. To expose students to a wide-range of perspectives, Meiklejohn also brought well-known guests to the college. One of these was R.H. Tawney, a leader in the English Workers Education Association and tutor in university extension, who spent three months in 1920 at Amherst.

In 1924, after leaving Amherst, Meiklejohn presented his views about the role of the book in adult education to a conference of the American Library Association. (2) He claimed that democracy in American life could only be built on education, and that education has to create 'the social mind'. Books were the major instruments for developing intelligence, for in reading books, persons studied how the great minds approached and solved problems. Through reading and the interchange of reading, a diverse people could become 'a single intellectual society', beause they found in books the meaning of their present and past experiences.

THE EXPERIMENTAL COLLEGE

After his resignation at Amherst, Meiklejohn moved to New York City in the summer of 1923 to write, lecture, and decide his future. Glenn Frank, then editor of The Century Magazine, became interested in Meiklejohn's ideas about the liberal college and created a committee to study the possibility of forming a new college. When Frank was appointed President of the University of Wisconsin in 1925, he found a way to create an experimental college within the university and invited Meiklejohn to head it. The New School for Social Research in New York City had invited him to join their faculty but he chose to go to Wisconsin instead. In the fall of 1927 the Experimental College opened, with a freshman class of 119 and a faculty of eleven.

In Meiklejohn's view, the two year college for freshmen and sophomores - 'the lower college' - performed a specific function in the educational ladder: it was designed to create intelligence, not specialists. The last years of college would be devoted to more liberal studies or to professional and vocational education. (3)

Through the liberal college Meiklejohn intended to train students to take responsibility for their own behavior. The basic instrument of this training was the book. As Meiklejohn put it: 'The whole procedure points forward to a mode of life in which persons, by the aid of books, are enabled to live in ways which are not open to their non-reading fellows, are trained to practice special forms of intelligence in which the use of books plays an essential part.' (4) This kind of education could only be tested in adult life. The liberal college should have equipped the college student to use books effectively in adulthood. Through the study of books, adults would come to know the significant values and problems of their civilization and how these values and problems were treated in any kind of literature.

The liberal college could not achieve its purpose by providing information about various subjects. Instead, the course of study achieved integration around a 'scheme of reference' so that students delved into those fields in which they should be intelligent. In the Experimental College curriculum, the first year focused on the study of Athens in the fifth century B.C. and in the second year on the United States in the nineteenth. In the summer between the freshman and sophomore years, students conducted a study of their home community, using as the basis the sociological study of <u>Middletown</u>, by Robert Lynd and Helen Lynd.

Students studied problems about which intelligence had been applied through books and they studied the problems in the real world about which intelligence was needed. The purpose was not the 'education of scholars' but the 'education of common men'. (5) Students were not called upon to do the kind of thinking that scholars did but the kind of thinking that men and women did in everyday life.

In June 1932, the Experimental College closed. Enrollments had declined because of the depression and the concerns of parents about the liberal social and economic teachings of the College. As a new venture, the College confronted internal university politics and administrative conflicts that could not be resolved. (6)

A SCHOOL FOR THE THINKING POWER OF A DEMOCRACY

When The Experimental College closed, Mieklejohn was 60, and its closing marked his second failure in the reform of higher education. In 1932, Meiklejohn and his wife moved to Berkeley, California so that he could write. He agreed to teach one semester each year at Wisconsin, which he did until 1938. Before moving to Berkeley, he had been approached by people in San Francisco to start a school for adults there.

The San Francisco School of Social Studies opened in January, 1934, as a private agency with four full-time and three part-time faculty members and 300 students who had been selected by an interview to ensure their seriousness of purpose. By the end of the 1935-36 year, the School had become firmly established. Meiklejohn continued to teach, but in 1936 John Walker Powell became the Director until 1942 when the School closed because of lack of funds.

The School addressed the unique needs of the city of San Francisco. The leaders, though, considered the School to be a national experiment in adult education. In San Francisco in the thirties a few families controlled the cultural life and the city was marked by bitter class divisions. (7) An adult education that could address these two issues transcended a local matter.

The organizers of the school had a social agenda, and they were not reticent in voicing their views. In July, 1934, six months after the School opened, a general strike closed the city for four days, and the longshoremen closed the port for 68 days. During the general strike, in an interview for The Christian Science Monitor, Meiklejohn's wife and member of the faculty, Helen, described the purpose of the school as helping people understand their social order. Things were wrong with capitalism, organizers of the School believed, and that abuse had resulted from the maldistribution of wealth and unbridled profits. Rectifying those abuses was a political task, but there was also an educational task: to help people understand the situation and to plan intelligently how to handle their opportunity for increased control. (8)

In 1935, the year after the School of Social Studies opened, Meiklejohn published a biting criticism of American society, explaining 'the inner failure' of Americans to achieve democracy. Presented first in 1924 as lectures at Northwestern University under the title of Education for Democracy, he then published them in a rewritten form as What Does America Mean? (9) To Meiklejohn persons had too often found the meaning of America in the 'outer' world, in the opportunity to achieve material success. The real meaning of America could only be found in the 'inner' world - in its ideals and values - particularly the ideal of liberty.

This ideal had been violated often in American history. To promote this ideal better, Meiklejohn proposed a new national policy in education and economics. Liberty as an ideal could not be achieved without 'life-long education for every one', so that learning would become 'a constant element in human activity - the attempt to know how living may best be done'. (10) For lifelong education to become a reality, newspapers, particularly, and other 'inner agencies for the interpretation of life' would have to become more educative. Everett Dean Martin held newspapers in contempt because they appealed to the 'crowd-mind'. To Meiklejohn, however, newspapers were indispensable in the pursuit of civic life. From newspapers citizens learned what people were doing and thinking, what problems they were solving, and what their interests and motivation were. For citizens to think intelligently required a dependable source of facts.

Meiklejohn called for a change in economic policy, and here he voiced his long-held animus against capitalism. He doubted that capitalism could be made to work, but its workability aside, he opposed it mainly on moral grounds. He found capitalism 'revolting as a form of human behavior' because free competition appealed to human selfishness. In capitalism, men were governed by an 'invisible hand', and in such a system men could not express their deepest commitments. Such a system was unsuited to democracy: it was so complicated that the common mind could not understand it. A socialistic program that involved everyone in planning and a scheme of action that the common mind could understand was preferable. (11)

Meiklejohn had thought deeply about the American social situation and the role of adult education. In the year the School opened, he used The New Republic as a forum to call for 'a national movement in popular teaching'. (12) Meiklejohn was grappling with the problem of the coherence of adult education. Around which principle or central idea should the movement be organized? Many agencies promoted the education of adults, but their activities were marked by their 'planlessness'. They had no teaching policy except to offer subjects in which students appeared to have interest. The basis for this national movement could not be vocational (there was already ample provisions for that), and it could not be equipping people to handle the new leisure, options already debated by others involved in adult education.

Meiklejohn called for the aim to be 'the creation of an active and enlightened public mind'. In American life, the most important issue was not economic or political; it was educational - how to promote 'the thinking power of a democracy' - but there was now no national system of adult education that engaged adults in 'the studying activity'. The 'teaching problem' of democracy was both difficult and important. Democratic government rested upon the intelligence of the people, but how the people should be educated remained the unanswered question and the unfinished task.

Meiklejohn had found examples of such national schemes in the Danish folk high school and to a more limited degree in the English tutorial classes. While these examples were helpful, the United States had, however, to find its own way. Work on coherence had begun by the 'powerful minds' of men such as Joseph K. Hart and Eduard Lindeman, but Meiklejohn did not find their solutions satisfactory.

The solution to the problem of coherence lay in book study. That was the American method. Significant work on this method had already begun. In 1924 the American Library Association began work on how to provide guidance in making popular reading more valuable and serious. Universities had addressed the problem as evidenced in the Great Books course at Columbia, the work of Hutchins and Adler at the University of Chicago, and the Experimental College at Wisconsin.

After his retirement as director of the School of Social

Studies, Meiklejohn continued his active interest in adult education, but he did not pursue further the problem of the coherence of adult education. Meiklejohn's colleague, John Walker Powell, took up the task. Had it not been for Powell, the School of Social Studies and the philosophy and pedagogy it espoused would have remained a short-lived, local episode in adult education history. Born in Duluth, Minnesota in 1904, Powell began his association with Meiklejohn while studying for his Ph.D. in philosophy and psychology at the University of Wisconsin. He was a member of the founding staff of the Experimental College and joined Meiklejohn in San Francisco to found the School of Social Studies. In 1942 Powell reported and interpreted the conceptual foundations and work of the School in School for Americans.

San Francisco had no systematic plan for educating adult citizens; in this respect it reflected the educational situation in the rest of the country. Many institutions had adult education as a minor activity but they did not address a social function. Institutional agencies were not bound together by any commitment to adult education as such. Teachers did not consider themselves professional adult educators; they mainly taught adults part-time and identified with other social functions or specific content areas. Decisions about adult education rested in the hands of administrators. Powell concluded that this situation - part-purpose agencies and part-time teachers - prevented the 'development or recognition of a single inclusive field of subject-matter which should form the curriculum of adult education'. (13)

Meiklejohn and Powell called for the study of social problems to follow the methods of the natural sciences in creating scientific objectivity. The natural sciences did this by the experimental method: any investigator starting from the same place and using the same methods would arrive at the same results. The conclusions resulting from the study would advance thought about the subject investigated. When people thought about personal and social issues, they mistakingly emphasized conclusions, not methods, and judged the results as right or wrong, good or bad. They did not inquire as to whether the treatment of the problem and statements about it had to be taken seriously by persons who wanted to be intelligent about the subject.

Using books as instruments of intelligence emphasized the mind at work: the books were used as a person solving a problem. What made a book important was not its historical status but its present usefulness, the importance of the problem it addressed, and the power of the mind working on the problem. Powell argued that the book possessed objective importance in itself, and in this process the teacher's role was to help the student see the objective importance of the book as he did. The teacher worked like a scientist in that he continually tried to develop his sense of the objective importance.

Powell put the issue directly. Can there be 'one education among our many schoolings?' 'Is there a subject field, a career discipline of the mind, whose content and method are implicit in the goal of the mind's struggle for maturity?' Is there certain content that an adult as a citizen should learn? Powell believed there was. (14)

In the democratic process, decisions of elected officials and administrators were subject to approval by the people. The dominant work of education was to create a 'public intelligence' focused on these acts: 'to make a kind of expertness out of the common sense itself, the common intelligence about the philosophy, morality, and politics of American living'. (15)

To create a public intelligence, teachers assisted students to be successful in translating knowledge into intelligence. Teachers drew upon every field of thought and experience to bring students into contact with every field of knowledge in which these vital concerns of society were being worked out. Since students worked full-time on their jobs, they could not become scholars in all these fields. They had to approach them from a 'frame of reference'. While teachers were expert in some field, they were, nevertheless, equal with students in searching for understanding and in bringing the resources of the students who represented many different fields of knowledge to bear on the problem under consideration. (16)

From one basic theorem everything else in adult education derived: education dealt with the adult as a thinking agent. Sociology, for example, regarded adults as material to be studied in their social relationships and institutional affiliations; training gave people tools but not the ends to which they would be applied. Educators dealt with persons as agents - instruments of their own purpose - and were concerned with the meaning of their action.

Men and women did not discover the meaning of their action in isolation. Persons needed a context of friendship in which to examine their conflicts and interests so that they could evolve different perspectives. Only the group method provided such a context. The group provided a different social context for learning than the classroom or the public lecture-forum followed by discussion. In these settings each individual sought his own purpose, but in a group activity the results could not be achieved by the individual alone. In group study terms, the group evolved a common method and mind as the group members interacted.

Meiklejohn and Powell wanted a method compatible with democracy as a political method. The group process provided a 'dynamic-action form' for realizing democracy in social behavior, 'education by experience in the techniques of democratic thinking'. (17) The educational task concerned how opinions, attitudes, and beliefs were formed in social situations that involved relationships and responsibilities toward others. Democracy depended upon 'group thinking': the ability to pool various intelligences without losing the variety. Members in study groups were to represent various occupations and social classes. When adult educators organized classes by categories of interests, age, occupation, and status, they perpetuated the divisions imposed by economics and social class.

Meiklejohn and Powell's 'instrumentalist' approach differed from the 'classicist' or the 'intellectualist' approach of Hutchins and Adler. Hutchins and Adler assumed that a student should be familiar with the history of western thought. To be civilized meant to them that persons had knowledge of the persons and ideas in successive historical periods that 'created the intellectual content of civilization'. Meiklejohn and Powell selected books for the purposes of the student, not what was in the mind of the author. They wanted to help adults understand the actions of persons in society through a common frame of reference. As Powell said: 'The emphasis is social rather than scholarly, structural rather than historical, purposive rather than appreciative.' (18)

A PHILOSOPHY OF ADULT EDUCATION FOR MATURITY

World War II brought the San Francisco experiment to a close. Powell served during the war as director of community services for the Japanese-Americans evacuated from California to Arizona War Relocation Centers. After the war he directed a three-year group reading program at the Washington, D.C. Public Library where he tested variations on the San Francisco program. Later he worked for the Ford Foundation sponsored Fund for Adult Education. In San Francisco Meiklejohn and Powell created an institution to further a value. Powell did not let it rest there, however. Out of that experiment he created a philosophy of adult education for maturity derived from a conception of the vocation of adults in a democracy.

Until Powell's Education for Maturity, no adult education philosophy had addressed the vocation of adults in a democracy. (19) Both the situation of adults in American society and the American approach to adult education required new philosophical thinking. Powell called adults homo multiplex because they had many roles but no center of integration. Americans built adult education on 'abstracted functions' - parent education, vocational training, public affairs, public skills - or served the interests of individuals as members of certain social categories - union members, church members. Adult education was a picture of confusion that had no institutional pattern, no accepted curriculum, and no professional leadership.

Powell did not want to change this apparatus of education nor did he belittle its accomplishments. But it was clear to him that this system - fragmentary and lacking a comprehensive strategy and method - could not address the issue of adult intelligence. Even in this diversity, however, there were some agreements. In the American conception of adult education, education and action were joined in a way that Powell believed to be uniquely American: 'This is that education itself is not a possession but an activity, a method of action and of modifying other actions in desirable directions. Learning, therefore, comes from experience in activity-situations'. (20)

Only education conceived as action created the conditions through which adults could understand the functions that comprised their adult role in society. All adults in American society shared a common role: citizen. Powell called this role 'the profession of citizenship'. The primary goal of adult educators was not to meet the needs of interests of adults but to equip them to perform the functions of citizenship.

A central tenet of the educational philosophy of adult group reading was that the adults had to do their own thinking. In American democratic theory the common sense of common people was to be trusted: experts should not be entrusted to direct the common life. But adults could not be left to their own devises. Teachers had a right, Powell claimed, to determine what the thinking should be about. Powell wanted to incorporate in adult education as a professional field of practice what had already occurred in many fields of endeavor. Practitioners in medicine, law, economics, and other professional fields had evolved a consensus about the standards of judgment which should prevail, and Powell wanted such a consensus to evolve in adult education as well.

Powell believed that through education as action - adult group reading - adults would acquire a 'common understanding of the philosophy, morality, and politics of American living'. Through this interaction with the ideas in the books and with one another, adults would evolve standards for the conduct of their life as citizens. They would develop an expertness which Powell called 'the profession of citizenship'. (21)

The point for adult education was this: adult intelligence was created in these social groups, it functioned in the context of these groups, and it must be trained and nurtured in that context. Rational intelligence - the mark of maturity and the profession of citizenship - was a social product produced by a social process. The group reading process compelled adults to examine their beliefs, values, and facts controlled by private feelings in view of 'the consensus of culture on matters of fact, on rules of reliable method, on judgments of value'. (22)

In developing his case, Powell worked within the philosophical idealism of Meiklejohn. In Education Between Two Worlds, Meiklejohn offered the idealist solution to the problem of how the student as an individual could enter into the experience of the human race. The student and the teacher came together to study subject matter and their experience then produced the social mind. They formed a social mind, a corporate mind, organized around some principle of knowledge in which everyone thought as one. (23)

Powell found support for his conclusions - the mind as instrument, communication as the medium, and maturity as the goal - in the branches of the social sciences and psychiatry that believed in the centrality of the interpersonal. (24) His sources ranged widely from gestalt psychology, to Freudian psychology represented by Harry Stack Sullivan and Erich Fromm, to Mary Parker Follett, and to Kurt Lewin. From these and others Powell formed his synthesis. Persons could be cured from pathology – reoriented in their relationships – only through communication in which they re-experienced the relationships that fueled their internal warfare, assessed objectivity, facts, forces, and relationships, and created new values. Practitioners in these disciplines - psychiatry in particular - had begun to recognize the group as an instrument of reorientation, as a means of freeing patients from the extremes of privacy by sharing in common group activity.

Adult educators had also recognized how the emotional factors - identification, transference, anxiety, hostility - conditioned the objective thinking of their students. In Powell's experience, when adults identified with the thinking process of a continuous group, three things happened: First, when persons revealed common experiences the anxiety of loneliness was lessened. Second, the group became a 'center of objective gravity' which persons used to clarify their own thinking by using the standards developed out of the group process. Third, the group also represented society in microcosm; as individuals began to shift toward more group-acceptable norms they also then shifted toward more socially-acceptable norms.

In the late forties Powell began research on the group context in education and therapy. (25) From 1949-1950 he was a special research fellow in mental hygiene in the United States Public Health Service and in 1951 research associate at the University of Maryland Medical School. In particular, he examined the 'science of group behavior' in the disciplines of education, therapy, and group work.

Group processes used in each discipline shared common features, but they differed in the emphasis on the goal to be achieved in the learning experiences. Therapy groups sought to correct emotional distortions resulting from disturbed interpersonal relations. Education groups attempted to correct methods of judgment that were inappropriate or irrresponsible and to help learners learn 'new modes of perception, appreciation, and performance'. Social work groups addressed inadequate social performances by developing skills in relationships. The groups differed in the attention given to the 'latent relational content' - feelings about relationships. Among these groups adult education offered the least occasion for verbalizing relational content. Groups, however, that dealt with parent education, mental health, interpersonal relations, and areas of conflict or change had to incorporate the feelings of members and their relationships to others as part of the content.

TOWARD A PHILOSOPHY OF PROFESSIONALSIM IN ADULT EDUCATION

In any short list of major works on the philosophy of adult education, Education for Maturity would have to be included, but Powell's achievement in this book remains unrecognized even now by adult education scholars. In the fifties Powell worked within the framework of this philosophy to address another issue: the value basis of the professional practice of adult education.

Occupational groups that wanted to advance their status in society often adopted the professional model. Taking the standard criteria of a profession, they assessed how well their group measured up to the several standards. Adult education was no exception. After World War II many adult education professors, doctoral students, and scholarly leaders sought through empirical research and logical analysis to determine the status of adult education as a profession. In Learning Comes of Age, Powell analyzed adult education according to the criteria of a profession, but he went beyond this to define the value criteria. (26)

Every profession attempted to conserve and promote the values of the society in which the profession performed a function. What values then did adult education serve? Adult education, Powell said, served the values of (a) free inquiry and experimental action and (b) study to enrich life, increase adult competency, strengthen civic participation, strengthen democracy in each societal unit, and develop individual responsibility and coherence of purpose and accomplishment.

Ideals governed education, and in each action of the adult educator these ideals were present. (27) The sources of these ideals were to be found in the concepts of the individual, the community, and the democratic process. The adult educator's values grew from 'the postulates of his profession'. The first postulate was that individuals exist, grow, and mature only in a society. The second was that the absolute requirement was communication: certain matters of thinking, acting, and feeling had to be made common and shared among members of that society. Adult educators served society through communication. They worked for the integration of community and opposed propaganda, prejudice, ignorance, anger, and fear because these were enemies of communication that subverted society.

Powell pushed the issue of professionalism in adult education further. Neither the administrator who arranged for courses nor the subject matter expert who assisted in preparing courses met his criteria of the professional adult educator. Adult education became a profession at the point of teaching and teachers but not at the point of administration, subject matter expertise, or unique method. The professional adult educator would have knowledge of some areas with which all educated adults need to be familiar but would be more than just a content specialist. The adult education professional would be 'a generalist of adult concerns and perhaps a specialist in some one of them'. (28) As 'a generalist of adult concerns', the adult educator assisted people to learn in company with other adults and fostered their courage in inquiry about the conditions of their common life. Only with such teachers could adult education become a genuine force in American culture, but this required the development of 'teachers of a wholly new order'. (29)

Professionals sought to awaken in others the same love with which they pursued their vocation: the criterion of the shared motive. (30) Adult educators wanted the learner to come to share the motives for learning they had and they sought to evoke that motive. Those who operated with the integrity of the shared motive differed from the motive of advertisers, salesmen, or even educational administrators. Educational administrators arranged the means for teachers to achieve certain ends, but administrators did not seek to create more administrators. The teacher dealt with ends that were valuable in themselves, and thus had value in serving other ends.

Beyond the integrity of the shared motive were other criteria for the professional in adult education to meet. First, they were to be attached to education through an institution so that they had freedom to devote full-time to their work and have professional standing. In addition to institutional and employment criteria, adult educators had to know the social, historical, and personal tasks that adult educators had to perform so that they could guide, inform, and equip the movement for adult education. In this regard, Powell suggested that adult educators make Albert Camus'

The Rebel one of their bibles they read often to think about their enemy: injustice, falsehood, and terror that create silence among men.

Too many adult educators, Powell charged, operated as though their activities were neutral or unrelated to the larger world of the adults they taught. All adult educators had as their central task the development of a working social intelligence. They should arrange every educative situation to be a force for maturity and to help adults reach decisions and take action. In this regard, Powell raised questions that he challenged adult educators to answer, and he offered some answers of his own. Adult education as a practice did entail skills - skills of discussion, group method, and community action - but it also had values that the skills serve. Powell called them 'skills of implicit commitment', skills that made a difference. (31)

A social philosophy of adult education should be unique; it should differ from the social philosophy of other social practices. Adult educators could test that uniqueness by deciding what influence they would exert through adult education if they had authority to do what they wanted in American society. What kind of influence does adult education represent? The answer to this question comprised the social philosophy of adult education. Adult educators, Powell maintained, did have some convictions though they did not take sides in deciding social and political issues. They believed that actions should be decided through intelligent study, persons should be emotionally mature, and social participation should be broad based. Adult educators were implicitly involved in major areas of social decision, but they were divided in their opinions about the role of adult education in society.

Those who sought to formulate a philosophy of adult education had no easy task. Adult educators carried out their work in many specific fields of practice, and were guided less by an articulated philosophy than by the traditions of the practice. To develop a philosophy of adult education, one had to work between a formal philosophy and many working creeds.

For the 1960 Handbook of Adult Education, Powell collaborated with Kenneth D. Benne, one of the founders of laboratory education, in a chapter to make sense out of the various philosophies of adult education. (32) By 1960 there had emerged two philosophical camps. The developmentalist school included fundamental education, manifested best in community development and human relations training, whose most important focus was group dynamics. The rationalist school operated under the banners of liberal education, great books, discussion, and the humanities.

The schools differed about the uses to which the learning situation should be put, whether for intellectual analysis, emotional analysis, or study and action as in community development. But Powell and Benne contended that all schools shared beliefs in common. All schools agreed that the adult mind was different from the child mind or the college mind. All agreed that education was concerned with guiding and understanding action and that between the academic and therapeutic ends there was agreement about the interplay of interpersonal and emotional aspects of learning. They all agreed that the most effective matrix for individual learning was the group context. All agreed on the individual learner as the agent of learning. All schools agreed on learning in terms of skills - education as an activity to improve other activities and to serve ends beyond education.

That the group method had been applied to adult education in the forms of adult reading groups, in community-action groups, and in human relations training did not mean that groups for study and action should be just another course offering. Rather, adult study groups restored the unity that had been lost through separate memberships and functions. One could not make the 'function of judgment' on the par with other goals; it was a special order all its own.

NOTES

1.   As a source of Meiklejohn's life, I have used Cynthia Stokes Brown, (ed.), Alexander Meiklejohn: Teacher of Freedom, (Meiklejohn Civil Liberties Institutes, Berkeley, CA, 1981).

2.   Alexander Meiklejohn, 'The return to the book', in C. Hartley Grattan (ed.), American Ideas About Adult Education, 1710-1951, (Teachers College Press, Columbia University, NY, 1959), pp.124-8.

3.   Alexander Meikelejohn, The Experimental College, edited and abridged by John Walker Powell, (Seven Locks Press, Cabin John, MD/Washington, D.C. 1981; orig. published by Harper and Row, NY, 1932), p.5.

4.   Ibid., p.16.

5.   Ibid., p.72.

6.   Brown, Meiklejohn, pp.33-9; Meiklejohn, Experimental College, pp.123-9.

7.   John Walker Powell, School for Americans: An Essay in Adult Education, (American Association for Adult Education, NY, 1942), p.4.

8.   Brown, Meiklejohn, pp.37-8.

9.   Alexander Meiklejohn, What Does America Mean? (W.W. Norton, NY, 1972).

10.   Ibid, p.234.

11.   Ibid., pp.231-53.

12.   Alexander Meiklejohn, 'Adult Education: A Fresh Start', New Republic, (August 15, 1934), pp.14-17.

13.   Powell, School for Americans, p.17; see also John Walker Powell, 'Thinking Power of a Democracy', Journal of Adult Education, 10, (October 1938), pp.365-70; John Walker Powell, 'Guided Study of Common Values', Journal of Adult Education, 10, (January 1938), pp.72-4.

14.   Powell, School for Americans, pp.136-7.

15.   Ibid., p.139.

16.   Ibid., pp.139-40.

17.   Ibid., pp.167.

18.   Ibid., pp.155-6.

19.   John Walker Powell, Education for Maturity, (Hermitage House, NY, 1949).

20.   Ibid., p.27, (emphasis in original).

21.   Ibid., p.34.

22.   Ibid., p.38.

23.   John Brubacher, Modern Philosophies of Education, 4th ed. (McGraw-Hill, NY, 1969), p.5.

24.   Powell, Education, pp.39-42.

25.   John Walker Powell, 'Process Analysis as Content: A Suggested Basis for Group Classification' Journal of Social Issues, 8, (1952), pp.54-64; John Walker Powell, Anthony R. Stone and Jerome D. Frank, 'Group Reading and Group Therapy - A Concurrent Test, Psychiatry, 15, (1952), pp.33-51.

26.   John Walker Powell, Learning Comes of Age, (Association Press, NY, 1956).

27.   Ibid., pp.231-5.

28.   Ibid., p.206.

29.   Ibid., pp.204-8.

30.   John Walker Powell, 'Some Philosophical Aspects of Professionalism', Adult Education, 8, 2, (Winter 1958),

pp.72-5.

31.   John   Walker   Powell,   (ed.),   Adult   Education:
Issues   in   Dispute,   (Adult   Education   Association   of   the
U.S.A., Washington, D.C., 1960), pp.5-7, 73-6.

32.   John   Walker   Powell   and   Kenneth   Benne,
'Philosophies of Adult Education', in Malcolm Knowles (ed.),
Handbook of Adult Education, (Adult Education Association
of the U.S.A., Washington, D.C., 1960), pp.41-53.

Part III

ADULT EDUCATION AS SOCIAL EDUCATION

Chapter Seven

JOSEPH K. HART AND THE COMMUNITY AS EDUCATOR

Some adult education theorists and institutional promoters found the unifying principle for adult education in the diffusion of knowledge and culture or in some conception of liberal education. Others such as Joseph K. Hart, Eduard C. Lindeman and Harry A. Overstreet derived their unifying principle from the social sciences. Their conception of adult education was informed by their understanding of the social sciences as a body of knowledge and as a method for promoting social intelligence. They focused their efforts in adult education on helping adults respond more adequately in their relationships with individuals and their memberships in groups, institutions, and communities. They thought of adult education as a form of social education.

The least known of these three theorists of adult education as social education was Joseph K. Hart (1876-1949). He stood on the periphery of the adult education movement that engaged the attention of so many educators, intellectuals, and public figures in the twenties and thirties. In his voluminous writings on different topics, two themes emerged repeatedly: the nature of the community as educator and the nature of education in the modern world. He had a lifelong quarrel with persons who equated education with schooling and separated knowledge from experience.

From experience he understood the meaning of small-town community life: the informal educational opportunities for children and youth and the mentality that rejected outside influences. Born and raised in Indiana, free from 'alien' influences, he attended college in the midwest and taught school in several states before enrolling in the

University of Chicago graduate school which granted him the Ph.D. in 1909. Except for a brief time in 1919 studying the War Camp Community Service program and six years as education editor of The Survey, Hart followed a peripatetic academic career.

His concern with community was more than nostalgia, for his constructive work on the community as educator occurred as part of broad social movements: the country life movement, the community organization movement, the adult education movement, and the New Deal social planning efforts. On each of these movements, Hart wrote a work of analysis, interpretation, and advocacy. The community educators have called him 'the philosophic father of community education', (1) and historians of the community organization movement cite him as one of the intellectual fathers of that movement. (2) His contribution to the theory of adult education has yet to be assessed.

THE COMMUNITY AS EDUCATOR

After a year as professor of philosophy and psychology at Baker University, Hart became assistant professor of education at the University of Washington in Seattle. In his responsibilities for teacher training, he adopted an unconventional approach. He made the state of Washington his laboratory and studied the life, work, and culture of the state. Hart reasoned that education was not the same as schooling. (3) Education did not have its meaning in what happened in schools but in what happened among persons and groups in the community.

The community in which schooling took place was a more powerful force in determining what was learned than the facts students learned. If teaching was to play any part in education, then the teacher had to work inside the experience of the students who were trapped by provincial folkways. In 1913 Hart published this position in a book he edited, Educational Resources of Villages and Rural Communities. (4) The book was intended to help community leaders develop a social understanding of the rural villages and communities in which they lived.

At the turn of the century, country life had come under scrutiny, more so by non-farmers and urban reformers than farmers themselves. Opinion was divided about the nature of farming, whether it was a business enterprise or a way of life itself. Those concerned about the preservation and enhancement of life in agricultural communities advocated the use of scientific methods of farming, better roads, improvement of the quality of rural community life, increasing cultural opportunities, and improved education. In 1908 President Theodore Roosevelt appointed the Commission on Country Life, an important event of rural reform in the early twentieth century. Issued in January 1909, the Commission's report on country life noted that 'all difficulties resolve themselves in the end into questions of education'. (5) Rural education was too bookish; it had to be more concerned with society.

In Educational Resources, Hart devoted only two chapters to education and the other 14 to aspects of community life, but to Hart the community had everything to do with education. The concern about how the community should educate its children and youth, how the community acquired an understanding of itself, and how the community allowed its citizens to participate in its life were simply parts of the same issue. The school began as a social invention to do what the community could not do in its old unconscious way, but it soon claimed responsibility for all education and ignored the common elements of community life that provided so much of the learning of children and youth.

Hart titled his chapter on education, 'The Community as Educator'. To him the community was 'the true educational institution' and the school a 'socially, supplementary institution' (6). As to how the community could be the educator, Hart offered only the general suggestions that the school should study how the community educationally impresses children, identify those elements that were 'sufficiently educative' and let those elements educate. For those elements that were weak, the schools then supplemented.

The 'community intelligence' necessary to solve problems of community life - industrial, sanitary, political, educational, moral, religious - could be developed and directed appropriately through social centers in the school, the church, or a publicly owned common building. These centers would provide a necessary mechanism for the expression of public opinion so that extreme individualism and extreme socialism could be avoided and power placed in the hands of the people and not in a special class or interest. The centers would then identify community problems scientifically through surveys about physical resources, human resources, economic activities, community health, local history, political life, outdoor beautification, social life, recreation, moral and social development, religious life, intellectual life, community life as curriculum of the school, and community activity in the administration of education.

In progressive philosophy and political theory, with which Hart clearly identified and from which he drew his intellectual orientation, democracy and the scientific method were inseparable concepts. His efforts were, he said, characteristic of the tendency toward 'a more complete social democracy' and a 'scientific view of the world'. (7) In aligning himself with progressive politics, he placed the primary responsibility of government not on protecting property as the conservatives claimed but on developing 'a complete moral personality' upon which citizenship rested. (8) The growth of social institutions depended upon 'constructive social intelligence'.

DEMOCRACY AND THE PROBLEM OF EDUCATION

From this contemporary diagnosis and prescription, Hart turned to an analysis of democracy in education from a historical perspective, which was published as Democracy in Education in 1918 while Hart was professor of education at Reed College in Portland, Oregon. (9) Even in this historical study the school as a 'socialized institution' and the place of education in the life of the community remained the central focus. The rationale for studying history, Hart argued, was to understand the problems of civilization and the processes by which these problems could be solved. Hart did not mistake the history of schooling for the history of education. As he said: 'The history of education is the story of the progress of the race in its search for new adjustments of its social life in the presence of changes in the natural and social environment.' (10)

In his reading of history, the conditions for democracy in education did not appear until the modern period. The primitive world shaped behavior through folkways, and the medieval world through belief in a fixed social order. The Athenian state in ancient Greece and the early Christian movement in the Roman empire were two notable exceptions.

New possibilities appeared with the 'birth-throes of the modern world'. (11) Religious rebirth occurred in the Reformation, shattering the medieval view that man had no existence apart from his institutional relationships. Intellectual rebirth came with the rise of science that replaced scholastic learning; the mind was now recognized as the creative agent in making the world. Political rebirth came through the American and French revolutions in which the individual became the center of reality and the masses were allowed to participate fully in government and determine the conditions of common welfare. Economic rebirth came in the industrial revolution that replaced a home economy with a factory economy.

In Hart's analysis, modern science and democracy reversed centuries of thinking. Psychologically, the fixed modes of thought were less close to reality than the impulses and feelings that grew out of human living. Sociologically, persons could renew their institutions and did not need authoritative control. Politically, traditional political formulations and doctrine of the supernatural order of society were less reliable in producing 'the good state' than human intelligence. Religiously, persons had to achieve their own good; it cannot be bestowed by an institution. Educationally, knowledge was being created and was changing, not pre-existent as in the Platonic universe. In brief, 'the inner forces of life and experience can be trusted'. (12)

These new ways of understanding the world called for a new way of thinking about education. In the medieval world, the fundamental educational question had been: what should I know? Knowing occurred as part of a fixed universe, and deciding what materials to include was the basic problem. But in the modern world, the fundamental educational question became: how shall I know what I know? Knowing occurred as part of 'an unfinished and incomplete universe of experience'. (13) The basic educational problem became the relation of materials to mental processes, this was the domain of educational psychology. To paraphrase Hart, what is the nature of experience and what are the fundamental processes by which the immature experience of the child becomes the disciplined and cultivated experience of the adult?

In this new understanding of education and experience, Hart placed Rousseau (1712-78) and Kant (1724-1804) at the center. Rousseau - a thinker Hart regarded as important but flawed in his thinking - emphasized growth from within rather than from external institutions. Kant held that the mind was central in the process of learning: learning consisted of creating and constructing an object. This new understanding advanced educational thinking beyond the solution of the realists to select the most valuable material, beyond the formalists to discipline a hypothetical mind into shape, and beyond the naturalists to free children from the artificialities of civilization.

A final event in the intellectual revolution that created the modern world and called forth a new understanding of education occurred in the nineteenth century. The theory of evolution began a new movement in the psychology of education. To Hart, the theory of evolution meant that the world was no longer fixed and its social laws immutable. Now the world had a history, it had developed. The theory of creation and its mechanical order had given way to the theory of evolution and a personal order. Evolutionary psychology meant that education comes in the process of living and that man's mind is an instrument in this process. Man's life was now integrated with the nature of the world; he was not created.

Clearly a new theory of education based on science, democracy, and a reconstructed community must be formulated to equip persons to live in this new world. In Hart's construction of this new theory, his debt to John Dewey was obvious. Eduard Lindeman would later formulate this theory of adult education in the framework of Dewey's pragmatism.

The educational task was to develop in individuals free intelligence and discipline, a self-discipline, not imposed from without. The educational process was inward, within experience. As Hart described it: 'The educational process becomes one of continuous growth of experience, continuous interaction of mind with fact, continuous reconstruction of experience, continuous development of control, and continuous discipline.' (14) In this new theory all spheres of life must be included in education so that education prepares persons for intelligent living. Finally, this new education could not be achieved without reconstruction of the community.

Hart defined education as the adult world giving its world to another generation. But an adult generation with undemocratic attitudes could not produce children who had democratic attitudes. The problem of democratic education lay not in training children but in creating a community in which children could grow up democratic - disciplined to freedom, appreciative of the good things of life, and willing to share in common tasks. Hart did not talk about adult education yet, but the creation of a community that nurtured democratic changes in the attitudes and thinking of adults was clearly the task for adult education. He had a vision in search of a concept, which persons in the twenties would call adult education.

THE COMMUNITY AS THE LOCUS FOR RECONSTRUCTION

In 1919 Hart left Reed College to study the results of the war in American communities and the War Camp Community Service. This experience continued his interest in the community which had begun in his educational work in Washington and Oregon and culminated in a book on Community Organization, published in 1920, as the initial volume in The Social Welfare Library, edited by Edward T. Devine. (15) The purpose of the series fitted Hart's abilities well, for the intent was to advance ways of thinking about social problems and not to examine techniques of social work.

Called one of the intellectual fathers of community organization by historians of the movement, Hart did not invent community organization. Community organization began with the Charity Organization Society movement in the 1880s and developed more fully through the settlement house, community centers, and social agency councils. When Hart wrote, community organization had already passed through several phases, beginning with a focus on community development (1907-14), to professional planning for co-ordinated services (1915-17), to community mobilization in support of the war effort (1918-19). In 1920-30 the emphasis had shifted to the efficient delivery of community services, interest in social change had declined, and community organization had become a subdiscipline of social work. (16) Hart, as did Eduard Lindeman, represented the segment of the field promoting democratic participation.

Hart remained true to his charge to advance a way of thinking about social problems, eschewing arguments about the nature and purpose of community organization in favor

125

of viewing community organization as a means of increasing democratic participation and assisting individual adjustment. Indeed, the issue was the survival of civilization. As he saw it: 'An old civilization came to its breaking point in 1914 and to its complete breakdown in 1918.' (17) American institutions could be rebuilt, but the danger was that the energies released by the war would be pressed back into pre-war institutional molds. The war had released unhealthy energies: profiteering, repression of civil liberties, and an unhealthy concern for 'security, sanity, safety'. And the war had also shown, Hart noted, that 30 per cent or more of young men were unfit for military service and that 33 per cent of male army inductees were illiterate.

In his analysis, Hart again worked within Dewey's pragmatism, identifying himself with those who approached community problems as a scientist developing tentative hypotheses of possible solutions. Every institution and service should be submitted to these two tests: What service does the institution provide to the individuals and the community? What provision does the service have for a more completely democratic community in the future? (18) Institutions had become specialized, and specialized institutions divided the community, developed their own champions and fragmented individuals who were pulled between loyalty to various institutions. Furthermore, at various periods some part of the community - property, the political state, and economic unions - had become the central focus in providing direction for the community as a whole. Hart's solution was more prophetic than practical: 'No institution can be trusted with the fate of the whole community.' (19)

It is clear that Hart moved against the grain of conservative opinion, those who believed that the order of society should be maintained by elite groups and established custom. Community organization, he claimed, was the basis of a new social order. A healthy social order required reconstruction; the theory of evolution had destroyed the conception of a stationary universe that did not change. The new social order was to be created and guided by social intelligence, which really meant the social sciences. The social sciences had, at least in his thinking, replaced traditional ways of thinking about politics, economics, and social ethics.

Pragmatism was the philosophical foundation of this new scientific way of thinking. In pragmatism, new levels of experience and patterns of living emerged from the process of reconstruction. The theory of community organization was pragmatism, pragmatism's method was to analyze scientifically how much of the old should be discarded. Alternative patterns of community conduct had to be hypothesized.

The social technology of community organization was the technique of community deliberation, brought about by organizing a group of people with expertise who represented the vital functions - not institutions - of the community. The group's first task was to educate itself in the purpose and method of deliberation and to develop hypothetical programs.

To realize the democratic community also required a new conception and practice of education. In each of his books Hart reworks the same themes in different ways. Here he claimed that in the democratic theory of education, education had the two tasks of helping individuals and the community become acquainted with existing knowledge 'in usable form' and to extend the range of human knowledge and application to solving human problems. Human knowledge applied to human problems was, of course, social science, which to Hart meant critical thinking.

Not only was a broader conception of education necessary, but education had to be extended into adulthood. As Hart said: 'In a democratic community education must continue as long as life lasts.' (20) A democracy could not survive unless adult citizens were growing in intelligence. Adult education had to be part of community organization because every program in any sphere of life demanded greater intelligence from the community. No knowledge should be excluded from the intelligence of the community. Because social and industrial conditions determine the outlook of men and women, programs of adult education may have to develop 'a definite movement toward community reorganization' to treat the problems that prevent a program of adult education for adult workers. (21)

Adult education had an inseparable relationship with the education of children and youth. Schooling was largely irrelevant to the life of the community, but schools could not change until the thinking of adults who were in charge had changed. Adult education represented the great hope for the reform of public schools.

ADULT EDUCATION AS THE NEXT PHASE OF DEMOCRATIC EDUCATION

From 1920 to 1926 Hart worked outside educational institutions as education editor of The Survey Graphic in New York City, but he also taught at the New School for Social Research and as visiting professor at several universities. He reported that he visited all 48 states and Mexico and Canada to identify ways of carrying out programs of community education in non-academic settings. (22) Sometime after getting into adult work and before visiting Denmark, Hart helped establish a school in the Pennsylvania highlands on the model of the Danish folk high schools. The school did not succeed.

In 1925 he visited Great Britain and then spent the summer in Denmark visiting folk high schools and studying the ideas of N.F.S. Grundtvig, the history of the folk high schools, and their impact upon Danish life. In Denmark he found 'the justification and the fulfillment of my own educational thinking of some sixteen years'. (23) He terminated his trip around the world and returned home to assimilate this experience.

In Denmark Hart found that his utopia of community education had become a reality. The Denmark experience restored his faith in education: when the minds of youth were given a chance, they could become intelligent, develop their own strengths, and contribute to the world. Hart reported his experience in a series of articles in The Survey Graphic, later published as Light from the North. (24)

What Hart found in Denmark was a school for young adults that enabled them to understand the meaning of their lives in its several aspects through a study of Danish culture communicated through the personality of a teacher. Students developed a life hypothesis and considered the forces in the community, including community and cultural traditions. In this conception, education was 'coextensive with life and experience', not schooling. The schools laid the foundations of 'self-education' in which the young Dane 'learns how to educate himself'. Such a belief in the plasticity of the human mind contrasted markedly with the mechanistic biology and psychology that dominated the thinking of many in the United States who believed that a child's destiny was determined before birth or in the first few years of life.

The folk high schools had played a key role in the

transformation of Danish cultural, political, and economic life in the last quarter of the nineteenth century. The Danish experience testified to the power of education to make a difference in the real world concerns of persons, and this educational result served as a magnet attracting Hart and other Americans before him. The folk high school had produced a civilization that combined both national culture and community living and the world of science and 'intelligent control'. It had released social intelligence - disciplined and free - to direct social change.

His analysis of the Danish movement was almost worshipful and certainly uncritical. In 1925, the same year that Hart visited Denmark and a year before the organization of the American Association for Adult Education, he also began to analyze the emerging adult education movement in the United States. What he observed inspired despair rather than hope. In a series of articles in The Survey his pessimism could not be constrained. (25)

American belief in the 'magic' of education as the cure for all of society's ills had produced a great system of universal education. To its shame, the system produced 'adults', adults who were complacent and had no capacity to continue learning. There was now no way to break up this kind of thinking and practice except to treat the products of the system: the adults. The inadequacies of the educational system made adult education necessary.

The interest in adult education sprang from several motives. One motive was the fear of the increased leisure of the working class. The leisure class believed they knew how to manage their leisure, but they were unsure of what the workers would do when they had been released from the discipline of long work days. Adult education's task was to help workers use leisure time wisely. But other fears about workers pervaded this interest in adult education, Hart maintained. For the past 40 years, workers had increasingly been 'alien' and they had 'ideas'. Adult education driven by the primitive fear of alien ideas could only be regarded as an extension of Americanization programs.

Safeguarding respect for the past and its culture provided another motive for adult education. Hart said that the creation of 'scares' and 'red menaces' was not based on real dangers but were simply attempts at social control. This negative position - based on fear of change - had been disguised as a positive program based on respect for the past or the love of culture. The intentions and the results remained the same, however.

Others promoted adult education of a particular kind in reaction to science and the scientists. These reactionaries were fundamentalists such as William Jennings Bryan who, Hart said, accepted no moral, economic, or political doctrine enunciated since 1890. There were economic and political fundamentalists as well as religious fundamentalists who distrusted science and had no tolerance for 'free teaching, free investigation, and free minds'.

A PROGRAM FOR ADULT EDUCATION

Adult education's place in the social sciences was recognized in 1927 with the publication of Hart's Adult Education in Crowell's Social Science Series, edited by Seba Eldridge of the University of Kansas. (26) One with a narrow view of education might wonder why a book on adult education would be included in a series that treated economics, labor problems, culture, international government, public finance, social pathology, and the American race problem. As his previous writings indicated, Hart put education at the firing line of social change; adult education was an applied social science. The book itself was standard Hart, a mixture of survey, advocacy, history, critique, and interpretation.

The problem that adult education had to address in the twenties had its origin in the industrial revolution. Building on themes from Democracy in Education, Hart described the United States as the culmination of the new freedoms released by the reformation, renaissance, science and other advances from the middle ages. But the United States experiment had been interrupted by the industrial revolution that broke the world and various social groups in two ways. First, the industrial revolution destroyed the custom and habit of organization in the method of labor: craft attitudes toward work. Second, in destroying craft attitudes it had 'mutilated' persons as individuals, destroying their range of diversity and imposing standardization on their productivity.

To promote industrial efficiency, the industrial processes were adjusted to accommodate the mental level of the employee. Work no longer provided stimulus for growth or pride. Industry became the central institution of modern life and compelled the reorganization of every phase of life. The other institutions, however, had not kept pace, and Americans lived with outmoded ideas about religion, ethics, economics, politics, and education. In 1922 the sociologist William Ogburn explained this phenomena in his 'cultural lag' theory. In Hart's explanation, the industrial revolution disintegrated the village but the village mind persisted.

World War I had many meanings for various groups, but to Hart World War I demonstrated the failure of education conducted as schooling. Public education, including colleges, did not produce intelligent adults, namely, adults with the ability to experiment with new ideas and to critique old ones. Schools had no connection with any out-of-school interests; they developed their own materials, methods, and testing procedures. Schools taught only what the community wanted taught, and the community did not want its beliefs and practices criticized. The schools denied children and youth experience in the real world by teaching ideas as though ideas were the materials of the world and not tools for understanding and controlling the world.

As Hart surveyed the popular and scientific literature, he found a variety of opinions, usually negative, about the ability of adults to cope adequately with the demands of life in the twenties. Americans had believed that intelligence would be produced by universal schooling, but that assumption had proven false. Hart's review of the literature revealed that Americans were confused about the status of adult intelligence and what could be done to increase it. Popular writers had characterized adults as infantile, and the intelligence tests performed on Army recruits indicated a high percentage of illiterates.

Psychologists had divided opinions about whether intelligence was determined by native inheritance or by environment. Opinion was mixed over how to produce persons capable of governing themselves. Some argued that the hope rested with increasing the birth rate of the better stock, and others maintained that the problem must be solved by an intellectual aristocracy.

Hart saw hope in the national movement for adult education, but certain tendencies in the movement caused him concern. The new movement was guided by the wrong objectives and psychology. The objective that guided the present movement was to complete the incomplete adult, to re-educate the wrongly educated adult. This objective rested upon the assumption that the social order was all right, something was wrong with the individual, and education's task was a matter of completing a person. While adult education had less of this fallacious psychology than public education, Hart feared that if adult education were to be brought under the control of public education then the 'standard formulas, standard technics, and standard psychologies of learning and achievement' would be imposed upon it. (27)

Already the new national American Association for Adult Education appeared headed in that direction. It had sponsored research by Edward Thorndike to determine, as Hart so condescendingly described it, how much longer it took a man 30 to learn some material than a man 25. To Hart, such an approach made adult education part of schooling, a process of standardized and mechanistic instruction. Thorndike, the most influential American psychologist, emphasized giving information to students. Thorndike regarded learning as mainly an externally motivated process of taking on habits without being aware of it. Mechanistic psychology permitted control of both the process and the end product.

A mechanistic psychology did not well serve an adult education that supported democratic participation. Only a psychology of growth - a social psychology - that helped the mind grow rather than form the mind could do that. A psychology of growth treated the mind as active process that organized the world and personality and regarded the individual and his experience as the reality of the world. To Hart, this psychology was eclectic, taken from many psychologies. While such a psychology had not yet been fully articulated, psychiatry and gestalt psychology were examples of this emerging social psychology.

Even in this treatment of adult education Hart could not escape his preoccupation with the education of children and youth. Correcting the failure of public education constituted the task of adult education, but adult education could not continue to recreate adults who had been wrongly educated in childhood. The cycle had to be broken so that youth came into adulthood free of the deficiencies that now crippled adults.

Hart had little optimism that adult education could effect much change in the way that adults 30 years or older thought. The belief that he expressed in Light from the North about the plasticity of the human mind - the ability to grow and change - apparently referred to young adults. Reforming public education required a point of leverage, but it was elusive. The school could only teach what the community permitted it to teach. Only as the adults who control the community became more scientific minded would the schools become more progressive. This openness could only come from adult education, but Hart remained unsure of the power of adult education to bring this about.

Hart did not offer a specific definition of adult education, but he presented a typology of adult education as forms of social control. The most regressive forms of adult education he called community drift and education by propaganda. Those who educated by community drift simply avoided criticizing the present condition, and most social institutions demanded this type of education. Education by propaganda was more active. World War I heightened the practice of keeping ready-made minds docile and passive through the newspapers, magazines, movies, and radio, the chief instruments of propaganda.

Adult education occurred in more positive ways. The dominant mode of adult education were classes for the un-educated or under-educated adult. Hart described this form as completing the incomplete - the task of undoing the work of the public schools - a necessary but regretted activity. Other forms received his praise. Self-initiated group activities such as the New School for Social Research, community councils of adult education, and the workers' colleges provided important programs. Hart held high hopes for education on the job. Most modern jobs did not require training of any length, he noted, but he held out the utopian hope that education would become part of the work place, and workers would share in determining their working conditions.

Beyond adult education as programs, Hart regarded adult education as an area of research, an instrument of reform, and as a function of community life. In 1927 university research had not yet begun, but research into the problems and development of 'technics' constituted an important element in advancing adult education. That research should include surveys of communities to diagnose community problems and prescribe solutions. An example of such a program on methods of social research and deliberation, not housed in a university, was The Inquiry, of which, he noted, Eduard Lindeman was a key leader. Beyond research, Hart called for adult educators to work for the reform of general education, a theme that occurred repeatedly. The problem that general adult education confronted was the adult with the 'finished' mind. Only through the reform of general education could youth enter into adulthood with an experimental attitude toward the demands of adult life.

At the highest level were the movements that recognized the place of education in the totality of civilization and treated education as a function of community life. It was at the level of education as a function of community life that Hart offered his constructive program for adult education. First, adult education began in adolescence as the process for entrance into adulthood. The Danish folk high school movement was the most significant example of this 'new education'. Begin adult education at age 18 when adolescents were poised for entrance into adulthood, still able to learn from the past and choose alternatives for the future. Other cultures had practices for entrance into adulthood; it was lacking in the United States.

Second, adult education could become an instrument for community life through the establishment of community education centers. The curriculum would evolve out of the study of the community under the direction of an education leader trained in the latest pedagogies of community study and the Danish experiment in adult education. Four general aspects would be studied:

(a) history as humanity's adventure from the primitive times to the present,
(b) literature and art as adventures in the expressions of the human spirit at various periods,
(c) science as the unfolding of more adequate ways of dealing with life and the world, and
(d) the community of the present as the results of this adventure.

Hart's Adult Education was his major contribution to adult education and its literature. After its publication, Hart turned to other interests. His achievements in this book were considerable, but his influence on those who would later attempt to develop a unifying principle of adult education - a philosophy and theory - was minimal. He performed the work of a critic, and he received a critic's reward. But to Hart, as well as to his contemporary, Eduard Lindeman, belongs credit for bringing John Dewey's pragmatism and N.F.S Grundtvig's folk high school ideas into the literature of American adult education.

NOTES

1.   Edward G. Olsen, 'Standing on the Shoulders of the Pioneers', Community Education Journal, 5, 6, (November-December, 1975), pp.8-11, 47.

2.   Michael J. Austin and Neil Betten, 'Intellectual Origins of Community Organizing', Social Service Review, 51, (March, 1977), pp.153-70; Roy Lubove, The Professional Alturist, The Emergence of Social Work as a Career, (Atheneum, NY, 1969), p.173.

3.   Joseph K. Hart, Light from the North: The Danish Folk High Schools, Their Meanings for America, (Henry Holt and Company, NY, 1927), p.xiii.

4.   Joseph K. Hart (ed.), Educational Resources of Village and Rural Communities, (Macmillan, NY, 1913).

5.   William L. Bowers, The Country Life Movement in America: 1900-1920, (Kennikat Press, Port Washington, NY, 1974), p.39.

6.   Hart, Educational Resource, p.9.

7.   Ibid., p.v.

8.   Ibid., p.95.

9.   Joseph K. Hart, Democracy in Education, A Social Interpretation of the History of Education, (The Century Company, NY, 1918).

10.   Ibid., p.14.

11.   Ibid., pp.191-2.

12.   Ibid., p.229.

13.   Ibid., p.248.

14.   Ibid., p.360.

15.   Joseph K. Hart, Community Organization, (Macmillan, NY, 1920).

16.   Robert Fisher, 'From Grass-roots Organizing to Community Service: Community Organization Practice in the Community Center Movement, 1907-1930', in R. Fischer and P. Romanofsky, (eds.), Community Organization for Urban Society Change: A Historical Perspective, (Greenwood Press, Westport, CT, 1981), pp.33-58.

17.   Hart, Community Organization, p.22.

18.   Ibid., pp.24-7.

19.   Ibid., p.177 (emphasis in original).

20.   Ibid., p.87.

21.   Ibid., p.115.

22.   Hart, <u>Light from the North</u>, p.xvi.

23.   Ibid., p.xvii.

24.   Joseph K. Hart, 'The Plastic Years: How Denmark Uses them in Education for Life', <u>The Survey</u>, <u>56</u>, 1, (April 1, 1926), pp.5-9, 55-9; Joseph K. Hart, 'The Secret of the Independent Farmers of Denmark', <u>The Survey</u>, <u>56</u>, 5, (June 1, 1926), pp.312-15, 340-3; Joseph K. Hart, 'The Plastic Years and the Open Mind in America', <u>The Survey</u>, <u>56</u>, 11, (September 1, 1926), pp.569-71, 598-602.

25.   Joseph K. Hart, 'Why Adult Education?', <u>The Survey</u>, <u>53</u>, (February 15, 1925), 595-6; 'Why Adult Education? II', <u>The Survey</u>, <u>54</u>, (April 15, 1925), 92-4; 'Adult Education and our Civilization', <u>The Survey</u>, <u>54</u>, (June 15, 1925), 348-50.

26.   Joseph K. Hart, <u>Adult Education</u>, (Thomas Y. Corwell Company, NY, 1927), pp.341.

27.   Ibid., p.195.

Chapter Eight

EDUARD C. LINDEMAN AND THE CULTURAL APPROACH TO ADULT EDUCATION

Eduard C. Lindeman (1885-1953) had many interests - adult education was only one of them - which he approached as a social scientist and social philosopher. (1) As social scientist, he believed that science should be used to achieve human happiness, but the increased specialization of knowledge divorced specialists from the non-specialist. As social philosopher, he sought to include the findings and methods from the social sciences in his thought and to find appropriate ways to apply these to social change.

Born in 1885 in St. Clair, Michigan, of German immigrant parents, Lindeman received his bachelor's degree from the Michigan Agricultural College at East Lansing. Graduating in 1911 at 26, Lindeman worked as editor, state extension director of the Boy-Girl clubs, and professor of sociology at the YMCA George Williams College in Chicago and at the North Carolina College for Women in Greensboro. In 1922 he resigned and moved to High Bridge, New Jersey to do freelance writing and private research.

Lindeman's book on The Community had brought him to the attention of the wider academic and intellectual community, particularly Mary Parker Follett. (2) In New York City Herbert Croly, editor of the New Republic, and Dorothy Witney Straight who had underwritten the New Republic, helped advance Lindeman's career. Lindeman became a contributing editor to the New Republic and worked with the Inquiry project. In this two year period of independent work, Lindeman wrote Social Discovery: An Approach to the Study of Functional Groups, published in 1924. (3)

In 1924 Lindeman joined the faculty of the New York

School of Social Work, a position that gave him an academic and financial base and a field of practice that he believed had great promise for democratic action. From that point Lindeman's career flourished. He wrote, lectured, and supported causes. His activities were numerous: lecturer at the New School for Social Research, director of research for the Workers' Education Bureau, consultant to the National Council of Parent Education, an organizer and eventually President of the Institute for Propaganda Analysis, director of the Department for Community Organization for Leisure of the Works Progress Administration (WPA), educational advisor to the British Army of Occupation in Germany, and advisory editor of the New American Library. In 1950 at the age of 65 Lindeman retired from the faculty of the New York School of Social Work. He died in 1953.

SCIENCE AND DEMOCRACY

Lindeman's pursuit of social causes did not spring from mere 'do-goodism' instincts. His efforts on behalf of peace, race relations, civil liberties, parent education, adult education, recreation, and planning rested on beliefs about the role of science in human affairs and democracy as a mode of life. In these early years, Lindeman experimented with and studied new social forms, presenting the results to a wider audience in books on community organization, social research, and social education.

In 1921 Lindeman published The Community, the results of ten years of community work and study of the community. Written as a textbook for college classes and as an interpretation of the community movement for the staff of the YMCA, YWCA, and community leaders, this book won him recognition as one of the major theorists of community organization in the twenties and thirties. (4) Lindeman found in community organization a philosophy and strategy for bringing democracy and specialization together in a working relationship.

He perceived that communities had come to be associations of groups or organizations that promoted special interests and performed vital functions. Formed to meet human needs, these organizations first became agencies with programs and then permanent institutions in the community. Individuals recruited from the community as leaders were often overworked and devoted loyalty to specific institutions to the exclusion of others. A fragmented community resulted. The answer to community fragmentation was a new social mechanism, community organization, that Lindeman called one of the newest of the applied social sciences. The community action process, partly sociological and partly psychological, ranged from a consciousness of need as the beginning point to compromise on a decision for tentative progress as the concluding point. So that the validity of this action process could be tested experimentally, Lindeman formulated principles of definition, assumptions, and operational procedures.

How to test experimentally the validity of action programs lay at the heart of Lindeman's approach to the social sciences. In <u>Social Discovery</u>, published in 1924, Lindeman explored the nature of social science from the perspective of pragmatic philosophy. Herbert Croly's introduction to <u>Social Discovery</u> placed Lindeman's approach in historical perspective. (5) The earliest social theory of Karl Marx and Herbert Spencer developed broad generalizations about the way society had to behave. They saw man's conduct as determined by external forces. A second group beginning with Lester Ward's <u>Dynamic Sociology</u> rejected that approach in place of a process of social evolution. They emphasized a science free from values in which social engineers brought to the service of social ideas the findings of research, but they stopped short of collecting facts about social processes. Lindeman, Croly claimed, represented a third phase in the evolution of social science in that he avoided guesses by developing hypotheses about social conduct that could be submitted to verification.

Lindeman wanted 'a pragmatic and a unifying social science' that would be a 'handmaiden' to those who searched for solutions to problems of social adjustment. (6) Only an empirical social theory was valid, but philosophy and science, however, were not divided by an unbridgeable chasm. The two tended to merge: 'Good science eventually becomes philosophical and good philosophy is scientific.' (7)

Extending the scientific method to the social sphere had also concerned James Harvey Robinson, founder of the New History, and William F. Ogburn, originator of the 'social lag' theory. They maintained that the social sciences lagged behind the physical sciences because knowledge was lacking. Lindeman disagreed. The real problem of man's knowledge was <u>how</u> he knows, not <u>what</u> he knows. But where to begin?

To use science as a method to advance knowledge about social life required that the sphere of the social sciences be correctly defined. The sphere of the social sciences was not generic man, but man in association, men in groups. 'Modern life is group life,' Lindeman claimed. (8) Persons had significance and influence only to the extent that they were members of functioning groups. Through groups, individuals expressed their dominant interests and worked to achieve them. With regard to this central reality of modern life, the generalized problems addressed by the social sciences - how man came to be what he was and why he behaved as he did - failed to advance knowledge. What needed to be studied were the specific problems of collective behavior: the activities that transpired between individuals as members of groups and the activities groups had with other groups.

Lindeman found an opportunity to study the psychology of collective behavior in farmers' co-operative associations organized to market farm products in response to deflation and collapsing prices for farm products that began in January, 1921. Lindeman used the farmer co-operatives - a new social form - to evolve a technique for studying all forms of group behavior. Other researchers had studied groups by searching for evidence of the mob-mind, by describing and classifying group behavior, and by conducting social surveys. Ruling these approaches out as unfruitful, Lindeman focused instead on the group's activity, asking what needed to be known about the group and its activities. In this case, members of co-operatives joined to advance some specific interest.

By identifying categories to describe these activities, unresolved issues in the operation of the co-operatives emerged and more adequate techniques of control could be devised. The issue of control of information and how facts were gathered resulted in co-operative fact-gathering. The issue of ratifying decisions or rationalizing what leaders had already done resulted in decision-making by participation of the constituents. The issue of the expert's relation with co-operative members resulted in what Lindeman called 'humanizing the expert'. (9)

Lindeman's results had profound social implications, Croly explained. Lindeman had produced a method to be used to re-survey major human associations - the church, state, industry, guild, and family - to discover what needs they satisfied, how well they worked, and under what conditions. A new social science would emerge, Croly predicted, to permit a continuing social audit of social activities by the agents who participated in them. Social science would be 'a body of recorded, interpreted social practice which would be taught in the form of a method rather than in the form of a social encyclopedia'. (10)

In 1922 Lindeman began work with others on the Inquiry project, an expansion of his interest in social research to social education. Sponsored originally by the Federal Council of Churches, the Inquiry project began in 1922 as the Conference on the Christian Way of Life to apply Christian principles to chronic conflicts. The Conference was not held, however. Some participants were more interested in exploring a method for resolving conflict than in applying Christian principles. The focus shifted then to inquiry about how any mode of social living in units could be made positive and integrative.

The Inquiry project lasted ten years, 1923-1933. Lindeman wrote the final report and interpretation, published under the title, Social Education. (11) In Social Education, Lindeman addressed already familiar interpretations of American life: 'urbanism, industrialism, and specialism' had thrown the democratic experiment off track, and now, in the third decade of the twentieth century, urban forces controlled and guided American life. Collective mechanisms had emerged as new social forms that now included all functional aspects of life. Individuals could not stand alone. They had to join organizations to have any influence at all, but once in the organizations, they could not act with a total purpose.

In this Lindeman saw evidence of the 'cultural-lag': the humanistic aspect of culture had not kept up with the materialistic aspect. The failure of value conserving institutions to adjust created an atmosphere for reactionary movements such as the Ku Klux Klan and anti-evolution forces. Below the stage of cultural-lag were the problems that institutions in the community had in handling institutional conflict and rivalries. The functional methods used by institutions became the focus of the Inquiry.

The leaders of the Inquiry project rejected the assumption that scientific research could easily be applied to achieve social goals. In their conception of social education, the new social forms of functional groups could be brought under control by personalities who had learned skills of participation and by institutions that had learned flexibility. Social education was a process and a goal, not predetermined ends and techniques applied externally to persons.

Questions about the origin and resolution of conflict could not be answered merely by gathering and reporting facts by quantitative research methods. As Lindeman explained, conflict was resolved by examining function and value, looking at how institutions and representatives of institutions evolved purposes and functions. This meant 'qualitative research' methods. The qualitative research method rested upon specific assumptions. The persons observed were involved and participating. The facts to be gathered were 'social', concerned with causes so that conclusions about their solutions could be drawn. These social facts consisted of attitude, opinions, and prejudices, that is, qualitative aspects of social situations. Because the facts had to be evident to the user as well as the researcher, participants joined in the fact-finding process. The facts became the common property of all, used to help participants clarify their purposes and to identify functions needed to achieve them.

A social theory emerged from the Inquiry project that Lindeman summarized in a series of 16 propositions to be tested by experimentation. Differences were a fact of human experience, and these conflicts and tensions were to be expected. These problems could only be solved when participants themselves discovered and recognized the social facts in the situation and not by 'the methods of naive positivism' in which experts made the identification. The expert might provide information and engage with participants in a learning process, but the only true learning occurred as participants gained insight and understanding derived from facts and feelings combined. Experts might work to bring about integrative possibilities, but the social goals and values emerged, they were not given beforehand.

DEFINING ADULT EDUCATION

Lindeman's reputation as an adult education theorist rests upon one short book, but he published several journal articles, which usually had been previously presented as papers or speeches at conferences. In these episodic explanations of adult education Lindeman searched for the essence of adult education as a new social form for experimental social education.

In 1926 Lindeman delivered his interpretation of the American adult education movement with the publication of The Meaning of Adult Education, a brief, evocative book now regarded by most adult educators as a classic. (12) It is not clear the reading audience Lindeman had in mind, but the New Republic press published the book. Perhaps Lindeman's audience were the cultured, educated readers of the New Republic. Nevertheless, he addressed the book, he said, to readers who sought no financial or vocational gain in learning and who were disciplined enough to engage in learning for the sake of growth and development. The boundaries of this kind of education were quite circumscribed: co-terminus with life, non-vocational, situation-centred, and based on the learner's experience.

Other writers regarded adult education as a means for the diffusion of knowledge, the liberation of adults from personal and social bondage, or the advancement of a social, economic, political or institutional purpose. Lindeman started from another perspective: the adult in the world. The adult, Lindeman believed, confronted the world in the form of situations, as occasions that required action. Adult education was a method that gave these situations a setting in which adults could discover the meaning of their experiences, analyze the situations, and plan actions to work through the situation.

Such a form of education had become a necessity. In the twenties adults lived in a world far different than previous generations of rural Americans. In this new world, science had made traditional guides for behavior obsolete, specialization had made knowledge the province of experts, and industrialization and urbanization had resulted in collective enterprises dominated by special interests. To address these realities of modern life, adult education had particular tasks. It had to link learning with the reality of adult life so that adults could find direction, separate learning from the control of specialists locked in narrow boxes of knowledge, and make the adult's experience primary.

Lindeman went beyond administrative and programmatic concerns that occupied adult educators in their daily work to probe the deepest meaning of this activity and the highest goal for adult learners: intelligence applied to life, exercise of freedom and power, self-expression, creativeness in the conduct of life, overcoming dependence upon experts, and making collective life responsive to individual needs.

Books such as The Meaning of Adult Education often obscure as much as they illuminate. Presented as a coherent system of thought, the ideas appeared isolated from their intellectual and experiential origins. Lindeman identified adult education as experimental social education. It was this form of adult education that was America's hope. And it was this form of adult education that he had in mind when he warned against 'Americanizing' adult education - packaging and promoting it as a product - before it had opportunity to grow naturally. His fears that the evolution of adult education as a social form would be aborted were derived from a view of adult education that was not commonly shared or understood, then or now.

The reason for this misunderstanding is easily located. Lindeman (13) viewed adult education as social phenomena, deeply embedded in social movements, in what he called the cultural approach to adult education movements. These adult education movements - folk movements with an educational base - emerged in response to some cultural disturbance. In the adult education movements in Denmark and other Scandinavian countries, England and Germany Lindeman found national case studies of this cultural approach.

His analysis of parent education in the United States illustrated the cultural approach to adult education and how the impulses that give rise to folk movements could be thwarted. More than any other traditional institution, Lindeman believed, the American family in the past half century had suffered from the effects of urbanization and industrialization. Concerned persons accommodated family life to this changing cultural pattern through a folk movement supported by an educational base: parent education. In their perplexity about how to deal with these effects, parents and teachers became aware of the need for new knowledge. They organized small collective enterprises in neighborhoods and local communities. Experts on family life created knowledge about families and disseminated this new knowledge through publications. Professional leaders (content experts) arose, followed by administrative leaders for the organizations that had been formed.

As part of a social movement, persons felt class solidarity. As part of their strategy, they engaged in continuing learning to understand their situation and to plan activities to bring it under their control. Experts could be used to assist parents, teachers, and other interested citizens to gain understanding, but experts were not permitted to dictate the solutions. As a goal and process they worked for cultural unity. Parents did not try to gain a competitive edge over other parents by the knowledge they gained. In the group process, parents, leaders, and technologists worked together to meet needs derived from the cultural 'unadjustment'.

In a social movement, such a process was not inevitable. Social movements could be aborted in two ways. Leaders with wisdom and foresight could initiate social programs, but the programs did not last beyond the stage of emotional arousal unless the people themselves became aware of their needs, possessed facts about their situation, and channeled these emotions into educative activities. Social movements were also aborted when they became part of what Lindeman called the 'technological world'. As part of a technical process, agencies concerned with family life made information available in non-technical language in newspapers and magazines and met individual need through giving specific advice. Parents, however, would lose the sense of class solidarity and control of the movement. If this happened, parent education ceased to be a folk movement. This was the 'Americanization' of adult education Lindeman feared would occur.

In the mid-twenties Lindeman (14) interpreted the incipient adult education movement from this cultural approach. An early attempt, perhaps his first, came in 1924 in a paper presented to the Southeastern Library Association at Ashville, North Carolina. Lindeman carefully distinguished adult education from other forms of education. Adult education provided for exchange of experience. As real education it had its roots in personal experience and not external authority, and it used the technique of discussion so that the teacher or leader functioned as stimulator and guide. Given these constraints, then adult education could only take place in small groups; books could be used but a new theory about the use of literature would have to be developed.

In this interpretation, Lindeman transplanted a European definition of adult education onto American soil, but it was entirely consistent with his developing view about the social sciences and social education. A visit to Denmark in the twenties where he studied the Danish folk high school as the agent for economic, political, and cultural change in

Denmark had made an indelible impression. Other Americans had also been similarly impressed, acknowledging Denmark as a model of how a democratic society could change peacefully through adult education. The other Scandinavian countries, the English workers' education movement, and the German folk high school movement after the war also provided evidence to Lindeman of the transforming power of adult education when connected to the activities of a functional group.

Adult education as a term included certain phenomena: all learning by adults did not fall under the rubric of adult education. Lindeman acknowledged that the American definition could not be borrowed from Europe - it had to evolve its own form - but it did share common features. (15) As conceived by the Danes and Germans, adult education had a special meaning that included the two aspects of

(a)   intellectual, cultural, and spiritual growth and
(b)   a folk motivation or end.

These two aspects - individual growth through learning in social medium for social end - were the generalized criteria for defining adult education.

When these generalized criteria were applied to the diversity of adult education in the United States, then many activities commonly called adult education were disqualified. Lindeman was not always clear himself about these distinctions, but in 1929 he carried the criteria to the ultimate conclusion. (16) Any educational activity pursued for degrees or any form of ulterior reward or which required entrance requirements or examinations would be discounted as adult education. By definition this ruled out vocational or professional education that oriented students to a body of knowledge accumulated to support specific trades or professions. These criteria also ruled out liberal education that sought as a method to liberate the experiences and ideologies of adults from bondage. Educational activities such as continuation classes, literacy education, women's clubs, and lectures were more examples of education of adults, not adult education. As he concluded, in the twenties the activities that counted as adult education greatly expanded as soon as foundations and philanthropists became interested.

Lindeman did not denigrate these activities he called

education for adults. In reality, he addressed the same problems of those in the dissemination of knowledge and liberal education camps: the problem of general education for adults. But he went beyond the humanizing of knowledge through formal and informal channels and the teaching of the thoughts of the best minds, ancient and modern. These advocates, to a large degree, identified the meanings before the process and used adult education to instil the meanings in the mind of adults. Lindeman, instead, believed adults discovered the meanings of life in the process of learning. In its essence, adult education was a method by which adults released their intelligence to handle the new social realities of the twentieth century.

In adult education adult learners brought in their experience some of the materials of education, which proceeded as a process of exchange between the teacher and the student. Adult education was a way of learning the relation between knowledge and living; it was not a process of acquiring the tools of education. Adult education was functional: it served the ends of individual growth. Adult education began with the situations adults faced, not with subject matter. The method of adult education was discussion. As Lindeman put it, 'organized discussion is to adult education what scientific method is to science'. (17)

As Lindeman had made a European concept of adult education more understandable to Americans, he also extended the progressive education theory of childhood into adulthood. (18) The central influence upon Lindeman's educational theory came from John Dewey. As part of a symposium on the philosophy of John Dewey and in commemoration of his eightieth birthday, Lindeman made clear his debt to Dewey. (19) His ideas about Dewey as an educator should be taken, Lindeman said, as his own ideas and beliefs about the nature of education and not just ascriptions to Dewey.

A theory of education was not the same as teaching and research, for many persons taught but they were not educators. Educators possessed certain indispensable qualities. In explaining these qualities, Lindeman described a normative theory of education: a conception of the nature of intelligence and the role of intelligence in human affairs, ability to see reality as a graduated series of values and not as a hierarchy, concern with method and process, and ability to link methods with goals.

Applying the scientific method to human affairs,

Lindeman posited education as a process in which learners - children and adults - acquire a method of learning that is so natural they apply that method to all their experiences in politics, economics, and social life without resorting to force or coercion. For Lindeman, as for Dewey, education was for growth in the direction of increased responsibilities - for the environment, for others, and for oneself - and the ability to experiment. Ability to use knowledge for social purposes constituted the test of the educated person.

ADULT EDUCATION AS A SOCIAL SCIENCE

In 1924, Frederick Keppel, President of the Carnegie Corporation, asked Lindeman and other experts in adult education to advise the Corporation about a possible role in adult education. Lindeman supported a study of adult education in the United States. In a memorandum, he made his reasons clear. (20) The movement, he wrote, had been retarded in its development because the agencies that promoted it worked in isolation, and these differences had obscured the real meaning of adult education. If adult education as a term were to be defined, it would have to be 'inductively described'. Because adult education was a 'social phenomenon', persons interested in social research as distinguished from educational research should be included in the study group. They should study adult education as 'disinterested science', using proper technical procedures and deriving conclusions and hypotheses that could be used as the basis for experiments. While the study itself should describe adult education and the interests and purposes it served, the study should have as its starting point two questions: What is adult education as a 'new social form'? What is the center of values that it radiates from?

Largely ignoring Lindeman's advice, the Carnegie Corporation commissioned studies on the institutional forms of adult education and funded Edward Thorndike's research on the learning abilities and interests of adults, research that was clearly psychological, not sociological. And the studies were descriptive, developing no hypotheses to be tested. Later in his career, Lindeman reissued an amended version of his agenda for sociological research in adult education. (21) Sociologists had failed to take advantage of the opportunity that adult education offered for research and experimentation. They had failed to do so, partly because such studies lay outside mainstream academic sociology, and partly because they would have had to deal with value questions and not just disinterested social science.

In Lindeman's mind, researchers would study the correlation of social stability, social progressivism, and adult education in Demark and Sweden compared with Holland, England, and Germany. They would examine the process by which new social forms emerged when adult education took root in a culture and the extent to which these social forms could be transplanted to other cultures. An explanation was needed for why the Danish folk high school was not successfully transplanted to the United States. Still another opportunity was to study adult education as a form of social education that worked for social change. An explanation was needed for how effective adult education had been as an instrument to shorten the 'cultural lag'.

An opportunity for Lindeman to address the relation of adult education to the social sciences came with an invitation to write the article on adult education for the Encyclopaedia of the Social Sciences. (22) It was remarkable for the clarity of his perception about the issues that divided the movement for adult education and his ability to cut through the rhetoric of the diverse positions to the central concerns. The term adult education as presently used was ambiguous and not helpful; no term that attempted to include all activities that went under the rubric of adult education could mean anything. His statement that there was some attempt to limit the use of the term to functional-group education and folk high schools - education related to a person's membership in a group - was not supported by evidence. Nevertheless, his analysis of adult education as a social science remains relevant.

In Lindeman's view, adult education intersected with social science at three points: general educational philosophy, content for adult education, and the pedagogical and psychological foundations. He disposed quickly of the debate about whether the aim of adult education should be individual growth or social improvement. Adult educators had erred in deciding how adult education was to be used. They should concentrate instead on the motives that brought adults to the learning experience. Beyond being responsive to the motivations of adults, adult educators did not need a philosophy.

As to the proper content for adult education, the debate over whether adult education should be cultural or vocational created a false dichotomy. Adult educators could solve the problem of content by determining what adults wanted to learn rather than determining what they should be taught. From a sociological perspective, the curriculum was derived from the adjustments that people were called upon to make. From a pedagogical perspective, subjects begin where adults had vital interest. From a psychological perspective, subjects should be compatible with the adults' intellectual development.

As to pedagogical foundation, there would be a variety of pedagogical methods, but the discussion method, Lindeman believed, appeared to be emerging as the distinctive method in adult education. It was the method of co-operative learning; discussion used experience as educational material, and adults could participate in this method.

SOCIAL CHANGE WITHIN THE FRAMEWORK OF ADULT EDUCATION

Lindeman knew from experience the reaction of conservative forces in the community when social mores were violated. His move from Greensboro, North Carolina to New Jersey in 1922 had been precipitated by a racial incident with the Ku Klux Klan. While in Greensboro, the Lindemans had let their black cook use their kitchen to entertain her friends at a birthday party. The Klan and the leading citizens of Greensboro became so incensed at this affront to convention that the college president felt compelled to release Lindeman. (23)

In the face of such injustice persons sometimes called for revolution to set right the intolerable social and economic conditions. Others determined in advance what they wanted people to believe and used propaganda to persuade others to adopt their point of view. Lindeman agreed with neither of these approaches. He advocated the process of re-education. Radicals and reactionaries were psychologically akin in their mistaking propaganda for education. Using force or propaganda for social change placed limits on what could be learned. Persons with faith in education emphasized the ways of learning, not its ends, the potentials of what could be known, not what is presently known. Social progress depended on interpreting education as 'growth from within rather than inculcation from without'. (24)

Evolving the social self through continuing education formed the bedrock of Lindeman's theory of social change. Not all persons in the adult education movement agreed with this position. (25) Lindeman called one school of thought the 'culturists': they believed that people should have education but they did not know when it might become useful. The second school, to which Lindeman belonged, contained the 'problem-solvers': they regarded learning as continuing, as co-terminous with life itself. Adults who believed in learning as cumulative used learning to understand themselves. A person who sought knowledge of self experimented with his behavior and acted upon his thinking. He subjected his behavior to self-criticism and used each moment and experience as an opportunity for learning.

Such a disposition toward learning had social consequences that extended beyond just the number of persons who adopted these attitudes. Such a process produced a 'social self', a self 'which learned awareness and oriented its experience through a conception of continuing education'. (26) As a consequence of knowledge gained through interaction with others, adults did not enter situations with their values fixed in advance of the experience. But in each situation they rediscovered their values. That is, they learn in action, not learn for action.

In the thirties and forties, Lindeman applied this understanding to many major issues of economic injustice, racial injustice, and national planning. In every position he consistently opposed violence, coercion, and propaganda as solutions. At the height of the depression in 1935 Lindeman convened the 'Swarthmore Seminar' to consider the 're-education of adults' as the educational solution to maladjustments created by the depression. (27) In the thirties Lindeman joined others in addressing issues of national planning. As an administrator in the New Deal program, he proposed a plan for creating a national policy on leisure. (28) He had no problem with planning as a method for social change, but he warned that succcessful planning entailed a psycho-social task as well as an engineering task; it depended on creating 'a new science of human and social engineering'. (29)

A better way than reacting to a crisis was to anticipate

it. In a symposium on higher education, Lindeman described the 'new' view of adult education as a 'mode of social adaptation'. (30) He returned here to a view expressed earlier in relation to parent education as a social movement. He wanted adult educators to recognize the tensions persons experienced in their social life and to make these tensions the object of study. If persons had already formed organizations to address those needs, adult educators should work to make the activities of those organizations educative. These emerging needs, these social tensions, constituted the curriculum for adult education.

Lindeman had learned from experience and research that recognizing cultural maladjustments and formulating strategies for change required knowledge and skills. He demonstrated his astuteness in projecting how education could be an instrument for racial understanding. (31) Persons began planning by identifying the stage at which racial understandings stood in their culture. Integrating blacks into American life and culture should be the basic aim of education for racial understanding. But for this minority group to achieve integration, they would have to gain economic status first, then experience in politics and government, and finally the right to their own cultural autonomy. Whatever prevented blacks from attaining these goals prevented integration. Blacks could not attain these goals without education.

Lindeman would never have asked whether the aim of adult education should be individual development or social change. Both aims were inseparable. Adult education connected with functional groups engaged whole personalities with their environment. For him, adult education could only have one unifying principle: helping individuals understand and respond intelligently to their situation. Lindeman began with the adult in the world and selected and organized knowledge from the disciplines to address the adult's situation. In this conception, adult education was social education.

NOTES

1.   My understanding of Lindeman's life and thought has been enriched by David W. Stewart, <u>Adult Learning in America: Eduard Lindeman and His Agenda for Adult Education</u>, (Robert E. Kreiger Publishing Company, Malabar,

FL, 1987); see also Stephen Brookfield, 'The Contribution of Eduard Lindeman to the Development of Theory and Philosophy in Adult Education', Adult Education Quarterly, 34, 4, (Summer 1984), pp.185-95; Robert Gesner, (ed.), The Democratic Man: Selected Writings of Eduard Lindeman, (Beacon Press, Boston, 1956); Gisela Konopka, Eduard Lindeman and Social Work Philosophy, (University of Minnesota Pres, Minneapolis, 1958).

2. Eduard C. Lindeman, The Community: An Introduction to the Study of Community Leadership and Organization, (Association Press, NY, 1921).

3. Eduard C. Lindeman, Social Discovery: An Approach to the Study of Functional Groups, (Republic Publishing Company, NY, 1924).

4. Michael Austin and Neil Betten, 'Intellectual Origins of Community Organizing', Social Service Review, 51, (March, 1977), pp.153-70; Roy Lubove, The Professional Altruist: The Emergence of Social Work as a Career, (Atheneum, NY, 1969), p.173.

5. Herbert C. Croly, 'Introduction', in Eduard C. Lindeman, Social Discovery, (Republic Publishing Company, NY, 1924), pp.ix-xx.

6. Lindeman, Social Discovery, pp.358-9.

7. Ibid., p.33.

8. Ibid., p.111.

9. Ibid., p.269.

10. Croly 'Introduction', p.xvi.

11. Eduard C. Lindeman, Social Education: An Introduction to the Principles and Methods Developed by the Inquiry During the Years 1923-1933, (New Republic, NY, 1933).

12. Eduard C. Lindeman, The Meaning of Adult Education, (Harvest House, Montreal, 1961; original publication, 1926).

13. Eduard C. Lindeman, 'Sociological Aspects of Parent Education', The Journal of Educational Sociology, 5, (April 1932), pp.500-7.

14. Eduard C. Lindeman, 'Adult Education: A Creative Opportunity', The Library Journal, 50, (May 15, 1925), pp.445-7; Eduard C. Lindeman, Workers' Education and the Public Libraries, (Workers' Education Bureau, NY, 1926).

15. Eduard C. Lindeman, 'The Meaning of Adult Education', Progressive Education, 6, (January-March, 1929), pp.35-9.

16.   Ibid.
17.   Eduard C. Lindeman, 'After Lyceums and Chautauquas, What?, The Bookman, 65, (May 1927), p.250.
18.   Lindeman, 'The Meaning of Adult Education', p.37.
19.   Eduard C. Lindeman, 'John Dewey as Educator', School and Society, 51, (January 13, 1940), pp.33-7.
20.   Eduard C. Lindeman, 'Memorandum on Adult Education', Carnegie Corporation Adult Education Memorandums, 1924-1926, Series II, 3.
21.   Eduard C. Lindeman, 'The Sociology of Adult Education', Journal of Educational Sociology, 19, (September 1945), pp.4-13.
22.   Eduard C. Lindeman, 'Adult Education', in Edwin R.A. Seligman (ed.), Encyclopedia of the Social Sciences, 1, (Macmillan, NY, 1930), pp.463-6.
23.   Stewart, Adult Learning in America, pp.39-40.
24.   Eduard C. Lindeman, 'The Psychology of Social Change, in Kirby Page (ed.), A New Economic Order, (Harcourt, NY, 1930), pp.357-71.
25.   Eduard C. Lindeman, 'Adult Education: A New Means for Liberals', New Republic, 54, (February 22, 1928), pp.26-9.
26.   Ibid., p.29.
27.   Eduard C. Lindeman, 'Introduction', in Thomas K. Brown (ed.), Adult Education for Social Change, (n.p. Philadelphia, 1935), pp.4-6; Thomas K. Brown, (ed.), Adult Education for Social Change, (n.p., Philadelphia, 1935).
28.   Eduard C. Lindeman, Leisure - A National Issue: Planning for the Leisure of a Democratic People, (Association Press, NY, 1939).
29.   Eduard C. Lindeman, 'Planning: An Orderly Method of Social Change', Annals of the American Academy of Political and Social Science, 162, (July, 1932), pp.12-18.
30.   Eduard C. Lindeman, 'New Needs for Adult Education', Annals of the American Academy of Political and Social Science, 231, (1944), pp.115-22.
31.   Eduard C. Lindeman, 'Next Steps in Education for Racial Understanding: A Philosophical Approach', The Journal of Negro Education, 13, 3, (Summer 1944), pp.407-13.

Chapter Nine

HARRY OVERSTREET AND THE DETERMINATIVE CONCEPT OF MATURITY

In the early twenties, Harry Overstreet (1875-1970) took a year's leave of absence from his position at the College of the City of New York to study labor problems. At this time, Overstreet was professor and head of the Department of Philosophy (psychology was part of the department for several years). As a result of the study he came to see the conflict between capital and labor as really conflict between the intelligent and the unintelligent. The solution, he believed, lay in the education of adults as well as children. Returning to New York City, he got involved in adult education, teaching on Sunday morning at the International Ladies Garment Workers Union, speaking at the Labor Temple and the People's Institute, and teaching courses at the New School for Social Research.

Overstreet came to attach great importance to adult education as a means to help persons live more intelligently. By 1939 his involvement in adult education had become so extensive that at the age of 59 he resigned his chair at City College to devote his full time to promote adult education by writing, lecturing, and working with organizations such as Town Hall and the American Association for Adult Education. His second wife, Bonaro Wilkinson Overstreet, an author and lecturer in her own right, shared this new career with him as co-platform speaker and co-author of several books.

Through his writing and lecturing Overstreet interpreted the research of the social sciences and translated these findings into applications for adult life in a language that the lay people could understand. In these efforts, Overstreet was clearly a popularizer. Critics of popular culture derided these efforts of Overstreet and others, objecting to the message of popular culture, as they interpreted it, that everyone could be happy and free from anxiety if they followed certain prescriptions or bought certain products. Ernest Nan Den Haag one such critic, showed his disdain: 'From Dale Carnegie to Norman Vincent Peale to Harry and Bonaro Overstreet only the vocabulary changes. The principle remains the same.' (1)

There was, to be sure, truth in Haag's observation, but there was more. Overstreet regarded himself as a philosopher who had made adult education the sphere of action in which he conducted his philosophical work: the work of mediation between the social scientists and the lay public. He was more than a disseminator of knowledge for popular consumption; he worked with social science materials to understand and improve human relations.

A PHILOSOPHER AT WORK

His efforts at mediation often ran contrary to popular opinion, but Overstreet did not shrink from controversy. In a 1945 Saturday Review of Literature article, Overstreet challenged the then commonly held assumption that Negroes were mentally inferior to whites. (2) Tracing the significant events in the history of this scientific controversy, Overstreet pointed out that scientific evidence did not support the position of an inherent Negro mental inferiority. The evidence, instead, pointed to environmental factors, the intelligence tests showed what communities can do to the minds of people.

In magazines such as the Saturday Review and in books, Overstreet presented ideas to the general public, but he could also communicate with scholars. It was in papers presented at the Symposium of the Conference on Science, Philosophy, and Religion in Their Relation to the Democratic Way of Life that Overstreet clarified his method and demonstrated his serious philosophical intentions. In brief, Overstreet believed that the social sciences had 'ethical import' and could be brought to bear in support of a philosophy of human relations. Anthropology, biology, sociology, and psychology had created a clear understanding of man and his world that discredited, for example, beliefs about national and racial superiority as unscientific.

The social sciences, in fact, had thrust a new agenda on philosophy: to create minds with a new outlook, 'a philosophy of maturity'. (3) Philosophers in the past had pursued other agendas. They had brought reason to man's thinking, prepared the way for scientific thinking in the fight between faith and reason in the Middle Ages and early Renaissance, and examined the assumptions of mathematics and the physical sciences. Philosophers now had new materials to work with and new tasks to perform. Now the social and psychological sciences 'are just at the point of emerging into competence'. (4) These sciences of man provided new evidence of the requirements of human personality; philosophers could no longer talk about psychological and social matters in an a priori way.

In performing this new task, the philosopher dealt with alternatives about the fundamentals of human relations. Overstreet defined problems in human adjustment as conflicts between extreme positions on a continuum. In the mid-forties, these were conflicts between democracy and fascism, isolationalists and internationalists, and racists and antiracists. In practice, the philosopher engaged in a particular kind of thinking in that he operated with two sets of facts. He had to have the facts about the issue in conflict, whether it be labor-management conflicts or race relations. But he also had to have facts about human nature, social structures, and human valuation. A philosopher could not, Overstreet said, remain cloistered with his books. Instead, he had a 'roving commission' to move among men to find out what their life is about and to help them live more productively. (5)

Overstreet had great faith in the social sciences to provide material for the philosopher in this quest for a philosophy of human relations. The psychological and social sciences were well enough advanced to provide 'a determinative concept' for the philosopher: psychological maturing. This concept, Overstreet believed, clarified the major problems involved in people living together; against this principle all the institutions of society could be tested. (6)

THE BIOGRAPHY OF AN IDEA

Overstreet's exploration of how the sciences of man and adult education could help persons live more intelligently

157

began in the early twenties with lectures in courses at the New School for Social Research to adult students. In 1924, Overstreet at the request of students at the New School taught a course on how human behavior could be changed in view of modern psychology. These lectures were published in 1925 under the title Influencing Human Behavior. (7) Overstreet posited as the thesis of the course that adults wanted to be effective in their environment - whether as writers, businessmen, or parents. And he took John Watson's psychology of behaviorism as the psychological system that could answer the question. In the first section of the book, Overstreet told how to gain the attention of people you wanted to influence. It read like a 'how to succeed' book.

Indeed, Overstreet was one of several persons who applied the findings of the new psychology to the selling of expertise. In 1928 he advised the Council of City Planners that city planning could be sold to the public - the public could be conditioned to accept city planning - if the concepts of city planning were repeated to them often enough. He advised the Council that people acted from their emotions, not from their reasoning, and their emotions could be channeled toward desired ends by appealing to their instincts of self-preservation, acquisitiveness, and competition. (8)

In Influencing Human Behavior, Overstreet acknowledged that these theories of motivation could be used to manipulate those with a product or service to sell or status to preserve, but these same theories could be used to free people from self-imposed or societal imposed bondage. A concept in behaviorism - the idea of 'habit-systems' - could be used to diagnose the public and its attitudes toward such issues as the emancipation of women and temperance. But applications of behaviorism did not have to stop with diagnosis. New and more productive behavior could be developed by helping people acquire an experimental habit of mind. People rejected modern change and inquiry. Overstreet called this the 'piety' habit of mind. He wanted to replace this type of thinking with 'use-value', an experimental habit of mind. Applying the experimental - the scientific - attitude toward social relationships would be, for Overstreet, the next great advance in civilization. (9)

In another course of lectures published in 1927 as About Ourselves, Overstreet applied concepts from psychoanalysis to the behavior of normal people. (10) Overstreet used psychoanalytical terms such as regression, fixation, hysterics, and phobias to describe behavior, but he softened the harshness of these concepts by characterizing them as evasional or contractive psychological patterns that blocked or retarded the growth of people.

Expansiveness, a basic personality pattern contrasted with contractive personalities, described a more healthy and mature type. Such a personality moved outward toward other people. Overstreet called the highest expression of expansiveness 'the intercreating mind' in which individuals united with something beyond themselves. Intercreating minds were parents who were being open with their children and respected them as adults, physicians who treated patients as persons, and citizens who refused to surrender their intelligence to interest groups.

From psychoanalysis Overstreet took the concept of fixation and translated it into a theory of growth. Human life, he claimed, was a 'continuous process of having to pass beyond certain stages', such as infancy, school, leaving school to work, and married life. Healthy life went by 'growth-stages'. (11) In the several regions of life - sexual, vocational, social, mental, aesthetic, and religious - a person's life either became fixated or grew.

Overstreet dedicated The Enduring Quest to the men and women at the New School who met once a week late in the afternoon to discuss the lectures he was giving on Life and Destiny. (12) In this book Overstreet examined the effect of physics and biology, particularly the theory of evolution, on man's view of himself in the universe. He rejected the view of materialism that man was simply 'a physico-chemical machine' in favor of emergent evolution. On the human level evolution meant that the human creature 'moves in the direction of more adequate functioning'. (13)

Overstreet coined the term 'ad-volution' to express his view of life as orientation to the future, a turning toward something provisional. Man, unique and conscious of what was superior, moved toward it. The philosophies of hedonism and stoicism were simply inadequate responses to life. In this view of the universe, only the belief in self-realization made sense. The most unique characteristic of psychological life was an active process of unifying. Philosophy, then, was not about thinking but about 'actabilities', a concrete process of life.

In the analysis of the sciences for a 'determinative concept', Overstreet recognized that these sciences and the technologies they spawned resulted in new social conditions. Adult education had a new social imperative. Overstreet characterized this age as scientific-minded, inventive-minded, future-minded, and humanistic-minded. In the twenties and thirties, persons used techniques to find facts and relied less on guess-work and traditional precepts. Scientists had replaced the priest and soldier as the ideal type. While the Greeks looked backward to the golden age and the ancient Christians to an unspoiled paradise, the key now was 'progressive evolution' in which the mind sought to shape the world in new forms. Man, and not just nature, was the object of scientific inquiry. (14)

American democracy was born when the farmer was the only specialist. (15) In a rural culture each new development took its place within a total community. In an industrial economy, machines multiplied and social relationships changed drastically. Knowledge became the property of the specialist, but such technical knowledge did not make the specialist an expert in social and political matters. A physician might be competent in medicine but incompetent in foreign affairs. Overstreet put the issue in a religious metaphor:

> Here, then, in essence, is the modern Fall of Man. We have eaten the tree of specialized and transformative knowledge, and we have had to depart from our rural paradise. The idyllic days are over. With the sinews of our mind we must now dig and cultivate until out of our hard mental labor we bring into being a new world of common thought and experience. (16)

To Overstreet, Americans thought wrongly and inadequately about many issues of central importance. No honest student of American life could ignore the warts on the face of democracy and capitalism: racism, isolationism, and economic injustice. In Our Free Minds Overstreet called upon Americans to take stock of the extent to which they had realized democratic values. (17) What about democracy, he asked, would inspire defense and resistance to the totalitarian threat? Americans needed to set their own house in order: they needed, for example, to christianize the economic order and equalize opportunities, raise the income level of people by extending public services, guarantee a minimum level of income beyond which people would not be permitted to fall, and create a mass-consumption economy that produced goods for the masses and not for classes. The problem, as he repeatedly said, was a failure of logic: people had not understood the requirements of the times. They had not recognized the interrelatedness of the human race.

THE EDUCATIONAL PROBLEM

Who was the adult that Overstreet believed needed education? As he pictured it in his mind, the average adult lived in a small town and had received his mental training in school which he left at 14. His mind was too immature then to grasp the significance of the facts about economics, politics, or moral life that he was taught. Left unequipped to study the important issues, at the age of 30 or 40 he read newspapers and magazines and went to church, but he had no opportunity to overhaul his mind. 'His mind, therefore, is, save in rare cases, a museum of immature fixations, snap judgments, picked up prejudices, and unverified 'hand-me-downs'. It is the mind of a child on the shoulders of an adult.' (18)

Even those who had the benefit of a college education probably did not examine or think about social problems. Even if they did, their training was now ten to 20 years old and the problems had changed. Such suspended spiritual and mental development was dangerous. In a democracy every individual had the two functions of earning a living and joining with their fellow citizens in deciding about their common life. (19) Adults were inadequately educated to perform their civic functions. They had received education for the societal function when they were too immature to understand its significance. Because of their immaturity, what they were taught about social matters had been greatly simplified and did not reflect the complexity of those issues as they occurred in adult life.

In 1925 Overstreet had noted that the newer philosophies of education, particularly that of John Dewey, had discredited the two-stage theory of life and education: the stage of preparation and the stage of living. In Dewey's philosophy, the life of children in school was not just preparation for something to come later; it was a life to be lived. So adulthood, Overstreet projected, would come to be regarded as not just the time when education was put into practice but as 'a process of continuing-education-with-living'. No longer could persons regard adult education as the chance for adults to make up lost educational opportunities. And in adult education, unlike public schools and college where teachers took care not to offend, teachers could encourage freedom of thought. Overstreet called for creating an educational slogan to reflect this new idea of education in adulthood: 'education without graduation'. (20)

Extending education into the adult years touched upon only one aspect of the problem, Overstreet believed. In addition to the age level problem, educational pioneering was required at the cultural level to equip persons to meet the cultural demands of industrial life. Science and technology had moved faster than people's ability to respond. (21) The nature of the new age required several kinds of new understandings. A specialized age required understanding to transcend specialities, an age of rapid change understanding to respond rapidly to change, and an interwoven age understanding to trace relationships. Such education had to be directional: develop wisdom in people for forecasting and planning so that the social consequences of events could be predicted.

The specialization of knowledge hindered citizens in their exercise of citizenship. Citizens did not have knowledge about areas in which they had to make decisions. Specialists in a narrow field could not make intelligent decisions about such issues as public utilities, tariffs, soil conservation, regulation of the stock market, or relief of the unemployed. Overstreet recognized the importance of specialization, but citizens should not feel helpless. They could break out of the confinement of their specializations by examining the broad social implications of their own specialities and by working with other specialists to examine the social implications of their specialities. (22)

Adults lacked a competency indispensable for effective citizenship: the competency of social thinking. That every profession or vocation required study and training was commonly accepted, but not many people believed that to be a competent thinker in social and political matters required study and training. But adults had to be trained to think effectively as citizens. (23) Specific competencies were to be mastered, and they were all aspects of the art of public discussion: the ability to participate, to detect inadequate forms of reasoning, to look at all sides of the questions, and to identify contradictions. (24)

The educational problem manifested itself in another

way: adults had few natural ways to be public-minded. Functions formerly performed by the old town meeting were now performed by many organizations in the community. These organizations usually worked in isolation from each other, uninformed about the activities of other organizations. Survey research in Michigan showed that many citizens did not participate in neighborhood activities; citizens tended to be private-minded, unconcerned about areas of public service. (25) Overstreet believed this withdrawal from civic life to be pervasive. When children and youth graduated from school, they were not given new 'fellowship situations' in which they could put into practice sportsmanship behavior. An adult had few opportunities to practice these social skills; spectator sports, lodges or service clubs were not adequate to promote these skills. (26)

A THEORY OF ADULT EDUCATION

To Overstreet's dismay, many advocates of adult education interpreted narrowly its scope and meaning. (27) They thought in stereotypes, Overstreet charged. Some regarded adult education as remedial education or as civic education, while others refused to include vocational education. Moreover, adult education had been afflicted with an image of 'soul-saving'; some hailed adult education as the hope of democracy. Another stereotype was that adult education occurred only in the classroom.

Overstreet, however, called for a greatly expanded view, for in his thinking adult education was inclusive, not exclusive. And he included in adult education such activities as parenting, beautifying the city, art, drama, music, and even vocational education. Learning occurred in libraries and museums: these were educational agencies as well as schools. To be sure, the field was diverse, but a theme united it: adult education of whatever kind and for whatever purpose had to do with connecting adults with knowledge. To make this connection was what distinguished adult education from other forms and levels of education.

In 1927 in About Ourselves Overstreet had begun to build a theory of adult education. The first element of this theory treated the relation of education to the age-period of adulthood. (28) Adults had ability and motivation to learn. New insights had emerged about the ability of adults to learn and their motivation for learning. Edward Thorndike's research on adult learning, which he reported at the 1927 American Association for Adult Education Conference, and reports from the Danish folk high school were evidence of this. The evidence buttressed Overstreet's belief that the adult was as capable, even more capable, of learning than children. Many things then taught to children could be postponed and taught more quickly to adults. They saw value in learning, and they had the richness of experience to learn rapidly and incorporate the new learning into their relationships and responsibilities.

As a second element of this theory, Overstreet worked on the premise that learning was only educative when it actually got into the habit-systems of people. Just as food had to be transformed to nourish the body, so a mental transformation had to occur with information taken into the mind. Traditional education, however, had failed to provide for this transfer of book learning to life. John Dewey championed a new education of learning by doing, which Overstreet regarded as useful for adults as for children. Learning that was acted upon required a situational approach. A presentation on the problems of single parents would not elicit much response. But the group would become alive when presented with the situation of one of its members, a widow, unlikely to remarry, with an eight-year-old son. Working situations prevented 'ingrowing mentality'. Overstreet called this ability to identify and tackle problems intelligence. Overstreet suggested that a curricula might be built out of these key situations of life. By acting intelligently - solving a life-problem in a new way - a person became a creator, bringing something into existence not present before. (29)

In studies of the Town Hall of New York City and the National Congress of Parents and Teachers that Overstreet conducted with his wife, Bonaro, they added a third element to this emerging but unsystematically organized theory of adult education: how could knowledge be unified in adult education. (30) Adult education as well as universities had to organize knowledge according to some principle. Universities solved this problem by ordering knowledge according to disciplines, but adult education took another approach.

An adult education institution such as Town Hall treated knowledge as one piece, refusing to divide knowledge into small segments. Town Hall was organized in 1920 by the League of Political Education to provide training for citizens. The Overstreets proposed, for example, that Town Hall might focus on seven interests which they called departments. (31) These would be the departments of social relationships, social criminology, propaganda analysis, proposed solutions, co-operative techniques, socializing environments, and cultural enrichment. An adequate study of these required knowledge of many disciplines, but in adult education the disciplines were not studied as disciplines. Instead, adults studied the disciplines to gain understanding of the interests they were presently exploring.

Adult education organized around needed psychological and social advances could provide a stimulus for change. Critical areas in American life demanded attention: the education of parents, workers, Negroes, and prisoners, to cite a few. In the twenties and thirties, adult educators debated whether all adults needed one kind of education or whether education should address concerns unique to particular classes or groups. For adult educators, workers' education became the test case.

The Overstreets stood for adult education that addressed unique concerns. They regarded workers as exploited members of society who had not won their full rights. Workers were the victims of 'class oppression and special privilege'. Neither the public schools nor state legislatures had made educational provisions to help workers understand their aims from the workers' point of view. Public schools followed a 'capitalistic middle class' position. From a traditional middle class position, workers education posed a threat. But from the Overstreet's vision of a comprehensive democratic society, workers' education was one means to bring about a new social order. (32) Later, Overstreet himself sided more with the moderate position of preparing workers for intelligent living and opposing the positions of the radicals who wanted to overthrow the system. (33)

The National Congress of Parents and Teachers, organized in 1897 as the National Congress of Mothers, represented for the Overstreets a new approach in adult education based on the principle of learning by doing. It also demonstrated how knowledge could be unified around a functional role and how learning and social change interacted. (34)

The National Congress built a national audience for every science - psychology, education, sociology, anthropology, medicine, nutrition, economics, and politics - concerned with children. At the first Congress and the meetings that followed, scientists were featured on the program. Articles in the official magazine presented scientific information and treated problems of the classroom and home in the language of the non-specialist.

To the Overstreets, both scientists and the lay public had responsibility in the diffusion of knowledge. But there were problems. Scientists focused on one aspect of human life - their speciality - and treated it as esoteric knowledge. They did not concern themselves with how these findings might be incorporated into the thinking of the public. On the other hand, the general public, occupied with the exigencies of daily life, was not always eager to learn about science. This failure of communication between the scientific community and the public had momentous consequences. When scientists did not inform the uninitiated - the laymen - then scientists remade the world without remaking the adult mind. (35)

To connect adults with knowledge required organization and leadership. This was the fourth element of their adult education theory. An opportunity to examine the organization and leadership issues of adult education came by invitation of the American Association for Adult Education to study leaders in adult education. After touring the country and conducting interviews with adult educators, the Overstreets published their findings in a small but important book, Leaders in Adult Education, as part of the American Association for Adult Education series on the Social Significance of Adult Education. (36) From the beginning they assumed that the issue of leadership was complex, and the study confirmed it. Considering adult education as part of the efforts that people made to gain control of their lives, they recognized that adult education could not be confined to programs offered by specifically educational institutions. Social and commercial institutions also undertook education to improve their functions. In these different aspects of adult education, leaders were differentiated as teachers and administrators, lay and professional.

The Overstreets recognized that educational leadership for adults was a new field about which little was known, but now the issue of leadership had become critical. The first generation leaders had sought to meet needs related to some aspect of adult life through programs of adult education.

Inexperienced in education, they implemented their programs through trial and error. But the movement for adult education had become so far advanced, widespread, and institutionalized that leaders had to be trained for this emerging occupational practice.

As important as institutional leadership was, the issue of educational leadership for adults ranged beyond the institutional level. The Overstreets recognized that adult educators had a social role that transcended their institutional function, for the American society itself had a stake in this new endeavor. Adult educators were mediators between the forces of social change and the forces of social conservatism. These leaders worked between the boundaries of individual development and social change to harmonize individual rights with social rights. Adult educators should assist individuals to develop within socially acceptable patterns. As mediators, they should encourage progressive policies emerging within the present system, without fostering revolution against the system. (37)

In this mediating role the teacher and not the administrator had the crucial function. It was the role of the teacher that revealed the uniqueness of adult education as an educational practice. The Overstreets called for the teacher to be a specialist plus, a generalist. As a generalist, teachers linked their specialized knowledge with the world of the adults so that the adults could see their ideas and experiences in the widest setting. Linking knowledge with the world of adults was important because adults suffered from 'experience deficiencies'. Their full growth had been restricted by their economic, racial, and vocational circumstances and geographical location.

In insisting that teachers be content specialists, the Overstreets challenged the obsession with method that pervaded adult education in the twenties and thirties. Adult educators had learned through experience that the restricted methods used in public schools with children did not work with adult learners. No knowledgeable person could disagree with that. But the Overstreets believed that some adult educators carried the concern about method too far. They had developed courses on methods separate from courses on content, and they had come to regard their task as that of providing a place where people could talk. But the Overstreets made their position clear. Freeing adults from restrictive methods did not, in itself, result in learning. Adults who came to discussion groups and pooled their ignorance or shared misinformation left the discussion group still ignorant and still misinformed.

MATURITY AS THE INTEGRATING IDEA OF ADULT EDUCATION

Overstreet cultivated his theory about psychological maturity almost from the beginning of his work in adult education. In 1940 in The Journal of Adult Education he presented a brief but carefully thought out explanation of maturity as the integrating idea of all levels of education. (38) The immaturity-maturity theory of education, he argued, was superior to two theories currently dominant in education. In the badness-goodness theory, the purpose of education was to make people good, to build their character. In the ignorance-knowledge theory, the purpose was to provide people with information about the world around them.

In 1949 he reaped the harvest of the years of intellectual labor with the publication of The Mature Mind. (39) The editors of the Book-of-the-Month Club recognized its appeal and offered it as a Club selection. For years the book-buying public made it a best seller. Beyond its commercial appeal, The Mature Mind represented an achievement of considerable importance in adult education: the integration of findings from the various social sciences into a single concept. In the maturity concept, Overstreet gave adults and adult educators a concept, much simplified to be sure, but derived from the social sciences, to use in measuring how well social institutions had promoted human growth. Adult educators could also find in this master concept a meta-goal which they should strive to attain in all their programs regardless of the subject matter under study.

Overstreet had formulated the maturity concept from a synthesis of five major psychological and psychiatric discoveries: psychological age, arrested development, conditioned response, individual uniqueness, and adult capacity to learn. These insights developed by Pavlov, Binet, Freud, and Thorndike - researchers with widely different approaches to human nature and learning - coalesced in Overstreet's thinking as the concept of psychological maturity. The social sciences yielded a common understanding of human nature and motivation. Overstreet described the maturity concept as a series of linkages an individual had to establish and develop throughout life: ignorance to knowledge, irresponsibility to responsibility, inarticulate to articulate, diffuse sexuality to specific and creative sexual relationship, self-centeredness to sociocentricity, and a world of isolated particulars to a world of wholes.

Adults found achieving maturity a difficult challenge, for the institutions in which they lived and which shaped their behavior and attitudes often promoted more immaturity than maturity. Overstreet measured the institutions of American society - economics, politics, the media, home, education, and religion - against the maturity concept and found that they had fallen short. Even though formed and constrained by these institutions, adults still had a 'margin for initiative'. (40)

Adults could free themselves from these constraints if they stopped looking back on childhood as the most exciting time of life and stopped regarding adulthood as an anticlimax. In the maturity concept, they could find the process and power to shape a new image of adulthood as a time of intellectual excitement.

Overstreet anticipated the idea of adulthood as a distinct stage of life. For him adulthood was a new and different life stage, the only life stage in which psychological maturity was possible. Adults had the right to enter this new stage, and it was the task of adult educators to take adults beyond the routine and familiar and move them into experiences that were genuinely maturing.

In 1949 no such program of adult education existed, but Overstreet imagined a community of adults coming together to realize their unfulfilled adulthood. What would these adults need to know? As a first step, they would want to see themselves through the eyes of maturity. They would see the world not as events over which they had no control but in terms of psychological factors - inner happenings - which they controlled. To do this, they would call in the experts with this knowledge: psychologists, psychiatrists, physicians, anthropologists, and sociologists. Instead of taking courses, they would use these experts to develop self-understanding and plan ways to put these insights into use. They would use these new insights to examine the ways in which they had been nurtured and educated in mature and immature ways, and they would identify more mature ideas about how the young should be brought up. They would also begin to do research on the effects of various institutions on maturity.

Possessed with these insights and sense of control, adults would be ready to make themselves at home in 'the great human tradition' they were exposed to in school but were too young to appreciate. As adults they could take a fresh approach to philosophy, science, religion, poetry, drama, the arts, and scientific inventions. But beyond just learning about these, they would practice creating and experience some creativeness in their own lives by composing or performing music, writing poetry, writing stories, painting, or sculpturing. In addition, they would take on some project for human betterment to give back to mankind something of which they had received. They would do research to get beneath the surface of specific problems. They would learn sociability by learning to play together.

Overstreet found the unifying principle of adult education in the concept of psychological maturity. Like Joseph K. Hart and Eduard C. Lindeman, Harry Overstreet, often in collaboration with his wife, Bonaro, drank from many springs of knowledge. Like them, as well, he saw adult education as the means to help adults understand their experiences in the world and to grow toward more mature and intelligent behavior.

NOTES

1.   Ernest Van Den Haag, 'Of Happiness and Despair We Have No Measure', in Bernard Rosenberg and David Manning White (eds.), Mass Culture: The Popular Arts in America, (The Free Press, NY, 1957), p.535.

2.   Harry Overstreet, 'Mind of the Negro: Notes on the Effect of Environment Upon Intelligence', Saturday Review of Literature, 28, (September 8, 1945), pp.7-9.

3.   Harry Overstreet, 'Next: To Build a New Outlook', in Lyman Bryson, Louis Finkelstein and Robert M. MacIver (eds.), Learning and World Peace, (Eighth Symposium of the Conference on Science, Philosophy, and Religion, Harper and Brothers, NY, 1948), p.285.

4.   Ibid., p.280.

5.   Harry Overstreet, 'Some Contributions of Science to the Easing of Group Tensions', in Lyman Bryson, Louis Finkelstein and Robert M. MacIver (eds.), Approaches to National Unity, (Fifth Symposium of the Conference of Science, Philosophy, and Religion. Harper and Brothers, NY, 1945), p.658.

6. Harry Overstreet, 'New Problems, New Philosophies', in Lyman Bryson, Louis Finkelstein and Robert M. MacIver (eds.), Perspectives on a Troubled Decade: Science Philosophy, and Religion, (Tenth Symposium of the Conference of Science, Philosophy, and Religion. Harper and Brothers, NY, 1950), p.547.

7. Harry Overstreet, Influencing Human Behavior, (W.W. Norton, NY, 1925).

8. Don S. Kirschner, 'Publicity Properly Applied: The Selling of Expertise in America, 1900-1929', American Studies, 19, 1, (Spring 1978), pp.65-78.

9. Overstreet, Influencing Human Behavior, p.222.

10. Harry Overstreet, About Ourselves: Psychology for Normal People, (W.W. Norton, NY, 1927).

11. Overstreet, About Ourselves, pp.38, 40.

12. Harry Overstreet, The Enduring Quest: A Search for a Philosophy of Life, (W.W. Norton, NY, 1931).

13. Ibid., p.75.

14. Overstreet, About Ourselves, pp.274-80.

15. Harry Overstreet, 'No Previous Training Required', Journal of Adult Education, 8, (June 1936), pp.241-6.

16. Ibid., p.243.

17. Harry Overstreet, Our Free Minds, (W.W. Norton, NY, 1941).

18. Overstreet, Influencing Human Behavior, p.194.

19. Overstreet, Our Free Minds, pp.157-65.

20. Overstreet, Influencing Human Behavior, pp.196, 197, 200.

21. Overstreet, 'No Previous Training Required', p.246.

22. Harry Overstreet and Bonaro Overstreet, Town Meeting Comes to Town, (Harper and Brothers, NY, 1938), pp.250-2.

23. Ibid., p.30-4.

24. Ibid., p.35-6.

25. Overstreet, Our Free Minds, pp.224-37.

26. Ibid., p.127.

27. Harry Overstreet, 'When Words go Forth to Battle', Journal of Adult Education, 10, (January 1938), pp.5-11; Harry Overstreet, 'The Elusive Thing Called Adult Education', American Library Association Bulletin, 48, (April 1954), pp.193-6.

28. Overstreet, About Ourselves, pp.166-71.

29. Ibid., pp.221-33.

30.   Overstreet and Overstreet, Town Meeting Comes to Town; Harry Overstreet and Bonaro Overstreet, Where Children Come First: A Study of the P.T.A. Idea, (National Congress of Parents and Teachers, Chicago, IL, 1949).

31.   Overstreet, Town Meeting, p.200-7.

32.   Ibid., p.236-40.

33.   Overstreet, Our Free Minds, pp.209-33.

34.   Overstreet, Where Children Come First, p.240.

35.   Ibid., pp.6-10.

36.   Harry Overstreet and Bonaro Overstreet, Leaders for Adult Education, (American Association for Adult Education, NY, 1941).

37.   Ibid., p.2-3.

38.   Harry Overstreet, 'Educating for Maturity', Journal of Adult Education, 12, 2, (April 1940), pp.117-22.

39.   Harry Overstreet, The Mature Mind, (W.W. Norton, NY, 1949).

40.   Ibid., p.273.

Chapter Ten

TOWARD AN ADULT EDUCATION TRADITION

The first generation theorists of new social science disciplines and social practices such as adult education evolved their new way of understanding and helping in response to a fundamental question. In the case of this first generation of adult education theorists, they asked: around what principle should the education of adults be organized? Is there an education that every adult should have?

Their most mature and reasoned responses - book length treatments - to this question appeared first in 1924 with the publication of William S. Learned's The American Public Library and the Diffusion of Knowledge and James Harvey Robinson's The Humanizing of Knowledge. The period of this first generation came to a close in the late forties and early fifties with the publication of Harry Overstreet's The Mature Mind, Robert Hutchins's The Great Conversation and the Great Books collection, and Lyman Bryson's The Next America and The Drive Toward Reason.

These early theorists worked on the assumption that continued learning in adulthood could no longer be left to chance. Educational movements begin when persons perceive an unmet learning need in society. In the case of these theorists, they diagnosed several. Some were concerned about the increased leisure of the working class, the lack of direction that citizens had, the extent of personal maladjustments, and the decline of religious authority. Adults lacked direction and were disoriented in a social order grown too complex for the average person to understand. They had little knowledge of the cultural heritage to guide them.

Others were deeply concerned about the extent of

repression and lack of openness to new ideas. New ways of understanding had come with the new social sciences, but many average citizens and leaders had not accepted the knowledge produced by this research nor had they accepted the experimental attitude of the scientific method. This knowledge was so highly specialized that the adult lay public could not make use of it.

Others saw the great dangers in the conditions created by urbanization, industrialization, and the growth of large organizations in which individuals had little freedom. The institutions of society did not promote maturity. Communities were fragmented by the presence of organizations promoting many interests - often chapters or branches of national organizations - so that organizations competed with each other for scarce human resources.

In grappling with the question of what kind of education adults should have, they were compelled to seek a unifying principle, some way of getting a sense of coherence, of seeing adult education as a whole. Some theorists gave more thorough and complete answers than others because they were involved in adult education in different ways and for different reasons. They all worked with a conception of education as a continuous process through life. Within this general conception, they evolved their answer within one of three unifying principles: adult education as diffusion of knowledge, as liberal education, or as social education.

An unplanned, but nevertheless, real social policy about the education of adults had emerged in the United States by the twenties. With the exceptions of university extension, co-operative extension, and public school programs, responsibility for adult education rested with individual adults themselves and with the initiative of various private and commercial institutions. Little, if any attention, had been given to how knowledge that did not serve special interest groups or institutional purposes should be organized and disseminated to the adult public at large. This task could not be easily solved. Adults organized their lives around occupational and family roles, not student roles, and most could only devote non-work time to study.

Those who worked within the framework of knowledge diffusion also recognized the importance of values, but others who located the educational problem in the absence of cultural values and standards took liberal education as the unifying principle for adult education. They wanted to restore to American life the values in the humanist tradition which they believed the social sciences had displaced or which had never become the possession of the 'common people'. Through group book study of the classics, the heritage of the human race could become the shared possession of every adult. In another variation, adults by engaging in group book study - both the classics and contemporary social science literature - would evolve standards of thought and behavior.

The diffusion of knowledge and the teaching of values and standards stopped short, for some, of equipping adults to manage their group, organizational, and community life. Drawing upon Dewey's pragmatic philosophy, the social sciences, and European examples, others centred their efforts on helping adults understand the psycho-socio dynamics in their interpersonal and social relationships. They, too, believed that adults should understand their cultural heritage, but they believed that such study made sense to adults only when conducted in relation to the larger concerns of their lives and not just as the study of a subject matter in isolation.

Obviously, the ideas of these theorists should not be compressed into a rigid classification scheme, for they shared many ideas in common. There are not, however, an infinite number of answers to the question of what kind of education adults should have. Just as scientists in the natural and social sciences work within paradigms - ways of thinking about problems and the framework in which the solutions can be derived - so do adult education theorists. For this purpose, then, classifying various theorists as to the unifying principle permits a critical examination of how they thought about unmet educational needs and how the needs should be addressed.

The literature in which these theorists either wrote or sponsored as in the case of the Carnegie Corporation was voluminous and rich in ideas. Some of the ideas warrant additional identification and discussion.

In the twenties and thirties adult education was regarded by these theorists as a new agency in society to meet the educational needs of a population that until then had not been served. They talked of adult education as though it were an entity in itself; it was, in fact, only a concept that existed in their minds. What existed in reality were the educational opportunities that institutions provided for adults or those educational experiences that adults planned and conducted on their own initiative with little or no institutional assistance.

Through what agencies of mediation - located in time and space - could such an ideal be implemented? The theorists - most of whom were also practitioners - evolved or called for the evolution of new agencies to mediate the knowledge they deemed most important for adults. Some agencies were proposed but never implemented: the library as the 'community intelligence center'. New agencies were created: the New School for Social Research, the School of Social Studies, and Great Books classes. Agencies organized to address cultural maladjustments such as family dislocations based their work on an educative approach; adult education was connected with the activities of functional groups. The Carnegie Corporation sought to impose the idea of liberal education on all institutions engaged in educating adults.

In creating adult education as a new agency, these theorists also had to grapple with the relation of adult education to the education that went before in public schools and colleges. The answer hinged on what purpose the theorists believed adult education should achieve. There was the theory of continuity. To prepare children and youth for education as adults, teachers should provide students with increased degrees of freedom so that upon entering adult life they would be prepared to make decisions about their continuing learning.

There was the theory of compensation. Adult education was the agency to compensate for the failure of the schools to educate adults properly when they were children and youth so that as adults they would be able to take responsibility of their learning and be open to change and new ideas.

There was the theory of adult education as an instrument to reform public education. In this notion, adults with closed minds controlled the schools and prevented the new ideas of the social sciences from being incorporated into the curriculum. If closed-minded adults became more open to change, they would, in turn, permit the incorporation of these ways of thinking.

As part of the larger issue of the relation of adult education to the previous levels of education, they debated the issue of the psychology most appropriate for adult education. Thorndike's research on adult learning ability provided the psychological basis for those who wanted to make adult education more efficient. Those theorists with other values who regarded the continued learning of adults as part of a civic role, as the search for meaning and insight, or as understanding of societal conditions, rejected this mechanistic approach to learning. They turned instead to the humanistic tradition, social psychology, gestalt psychology, or psychiatry.

They were divided, also, over the relationship of adult education to society. Even those who regarded adult education as the study of books in classes anticipated social consequences as a result of the learning. Experiences in liberal education should produce adults who were tolerant, open-minded, and would not succumb to propaganda. Social change then was simply the changes that occurred when adults had become persons of reasonableness.

Others saw a more direct relationship between adult education and social change. Adult education was more than studying the recorded experiences of the human race and the best thinking of intelligent persons as written in books. In the thinking of the theorists who regarded adult education as social education and others such as Bryson, Meiklejohn, and Powell, the content of adult education included the study of social institutions and their effects on the lives of adults. Adult education was a method for examining experience, studying actual situations in organizations and the community, and deciding what action should be taken.

In the evolution of adult education as a new agency, the issue of leadership became an important matter. In the development of organizational forms, a specialized administrative personnel always emerges. In the field of adult education, the administrative personnel are often regarded as the professionals. Several of the theorists took a different approach. The point at which personnel in adult education could be considered professional was not at the administrative level but at the teaching level. Professionals in adult education possessed specialized knowledge - disciplined based knowledge - which they applied to adult situations, normally, but not always, in a group context.

At one level, those who possessed specialized knowledge conveyed that knowledge to the adult lay public through a new literary form: knowledge interpreted for the lay persons in a small, readable book. At another level, the expert worked with adults in a group setting to assist them to understand the specialized knowledge, to interpret that knowledge, and to apply it to their lives. The intent was to make the knowledge a part of their thought processes and emotions. At still another level, the expert as adult educator would begin with the experiences or the situations of adults, assist them to understand what their interests were, draw upon relevant knowledge or experts for new information, and formulate with them a plan of action.

Each of the theorists saw adult education in a historical context. Some saw adult education in the short term context as a new form to address educational needs created by the conditions of leisure, decline of religious authority, increasing complexity of modern life, and incessant propaganda. Others regarded their program of adult education - especially those who drew their inspiration from the humanistic tradition of the Greeks and the synthesis of the Catholic church in the Middle Ages - as an attempt to restore an emphasis that had been lost by the rise of the common man or by the dominance of the social sciences.

A longer view of history permeated the thinking of others. Beginning with the Renaissance, a succession of revolutions had swept the western world that had resulted in increased freedom for individuals and a new way of thinking about the world - experimental science. Adult education, seen in this longer view of history, was another episode in this succession of revolutions. Among the adult education theorists, adult education in this historical perspective had two meanings.

One group was concerned about the 'democratization' of knowledge and culture. In an oversimplified statement of their position, it can be said that they wanted adults in every walk of life and social level - and not just the elite - to have access to specialized knowledge and the cultural products of art, literature, music, and drama. Adult education was a means for the dissemination of knowledge and cultural products to the masses.

For another group adult education was the means to diffuse the methods of the experimental social sciences. Just as social scientists conducted research on problems of their discipline, so these adult educators wanted adults to take an experimental approach to the organizations and communities in which they lived. Adults would study social institutions to assess the extent to which they performed adequately the function they were intended to perform. If they did not, the institutions were to be reformed. Just as adults learned by the reconstruction of experience, so did institutions and communities.

For persons now who view adult education from the

outside, and for many who view it from the inside, the field of adult education appears to be without a pattern. That may well be true, for adult education from an institutional perspective is simply a process that organizations use to make connection with prospective adult learners, whether they be employees, members, customers, or members of the community at large. The values guiding that educational process are usually derived from a specific field of practice or the purposes of the sponsoring institution.

Others - always very few in number - wrestle with the more fundamental question of what kind of education adults should have. They are concerned with societal needs and purposes, and not necessarily those of institutions. Always they work to find a unifying principle - usually with a vision of the good society - to give meaning and coherence to their efforts. Beginning in the second decade of this century and extending to the early fifties a few persons addressed this fundamental question. Their answer constitutes the adult education tradition in the United States.

INDEX